Living the Writer's Life

ERIC MAISEL, PH.D.

D0971403

Watson-Guptill Publications
New York

Published in 1999 by Watson-Guptill Publications, a division of BPI Communications, Inc., 1515 Broadway, New York, NY 10036-8986

Acquiring editor: Dale Ramsey
Copyeditor: Lester Strong
Designer: Cheryl Viker
Production manager: Ellen Greene

Cover image: Stephanie Garcia / nonstock; printed with permission

Library of Congress Cataloging-in-Publication Data for this title can be obtained by writing to the Library of Congress, Washington, D.C. 20540

ISBN 0-8230-8848-0

Manufactured in the United States of America

1 2 3 4 5 6 7 8 9 / 03 02 01 00 99

For Ann, this writer's best friend

Acknowledgments

First, I'd like to thank the people who contributed original pieces
to this book: Roccie Austin Hill, Steve Mettee, Alan Rinzler, W. Joe Innis,
Melissa Bay Mathis, Maire Farrington, Donna Levin, Susanne West,
Jan Johnson Drantell, Ed Hooks, and "Anonymous." Your contributions
have enriched *Living the Writer's Life* immeasurably.

Next, I express thanks to my editor, Dale Ramsey,
and all the folks at Watson-Guptill Publications who helped make
this book a reality and who are helping it reach its audience.

I'm especially indebted to my writing clients, to the writers I meet
at workshops and conferences, and to the writers who take
the time to correspond with me, all of whom educate me about
what it means to be a writer.

I'd also like to say thank you to the artists in my life:
Ann, David, Natalya, and Kira.

Contents

Introduction

This book is meant to accompany you through a lifetime of writing. I've been writing for thirty years and I've taught writing at the college level and counseled writers as a therapist and creativity consultant for the past fifteen years. I'd like to communicate some of the lessons I've learned during that time, provide you with some advice and exercises, and help you handle the many obstacles and challenges that come with the writing life. I hope that what I have to say both prepares you for that life and offers you some comfort as you live it.

No one knows if a writer is made or born or whether writers share a single common personality profile. My own experience is that when people who do not consider themselves writers but who want or need to write understand what's required of them, they start to write well and become writers. The ability to write, like the ability to speak or to communicate our thoughts, is a basic feature of the species. When people claim to be uncreative or incapable of writing they are always saying something about the emotional and practical difficulties they face in life, and not anything about their talents or abilities. Probably the only thing that distinguishes the writer from the nonwriter is that the writer is motivated or compelled to write and that she has taken the plunge and begun writing.

But perhaps that motivation or compulsion does distinguish the writer from the nonwriter: perhaps that's the special quality a writer is born with. I doubt that, though. What seems more true to me is that anyone who has ever loved a book also harbors the dream to write one. But the opportunity to write is so reduced in most people's lives, both as a psychological matter and a practical one, that they lose their motivation. The young child will write stories, until that natural ability is squelched. Everyone is born motivated to write but most people become unmotivated over time through unfortunate circumstance.

So a very large class of people is created: would-be writers who dream about writing but who do not write much or at all. If that is you, this book is geared to your needs; my hope is that you become the full-fledged writer you hope to become. But that simple invitation comes with several warnings. Writing is as easy and natural as speaking, but writing well is extremely hard, just as gathering one's thoughts and effectively communicating them is extremely hard. How many teachers, even those who have been teaching for a long time and know their subject well, lecture brilliantly? Very few. Why? Because they do not take the time or make the effort to prepare brilliant lectures. Could they if they tried? I think so. If they put their hearts and minds into it, they could wake up their students.

That is warning one, that writing well requires real effort. Warning two has to do with the psychological and emotional problems that are part of the writing life. Some of these problems may be constitutional but others arise as a result of trying to write, trying to sell, and trying to live as a writer. I don't think it's possible to know whether a given writer was born depressed or has become depressed because his first two novels haven't sold, but that failure to sell is a contributing factor as large as a house. Nor is it possible to know to what extent a person's self-esteem is eroded by insulting criticism and repeated rejections, but that it must be eroded seems certain. It is fair to say that the writing life, like any creative life, comes with its share of emotional knocks built right in.

Warning three has to do with the realities of the marketplace. Most young writers and many older writers do not want to think about the financial realities of living the writing life, because to see them clearly might sap their motivational strength and remind them that a lifetime of unwanted day jobs awaits them. Is it better to think honestly about how much money writers make and perhaps give up, or is it better to avoid thinking about it and live the insecure, helter-skelter life that usually follows a decision to pursue writing seriously? There is no really good answer to this important question.

The realities of the marketplace are daunting and you'll want to consider how to handle them as effectively as possible—primarily by writing books that are wanted and by networking a lot. Or you might consider creating a life that pays the rent and that also allows you to write, a life built around teaching full-time, editing part-time, writing technical manuals or corporate reports, becoming a lawyer or a sea captain, or marrying someone with a salary. Or you might decide to wait on tables and write your poetry, novels, or stage plays all through your twenties and thirties, accepting the contours of that arduous life as best you can (after forty the emotional difficulties become really grave). These are the actual marketplace dilemmas of working writers and they rarely get completely solved or put to rest.

I would like you to understand as early as possible in your writing life that these three challenges exist, even if you decide to ignore them. If you're at least aware of their existence—that good writing is hard work, that emotional problems come with the territory, and that only a few writers manage to pay the rent from their writing income—you can keep a mental tally just out of conscious awareness, readying yourself for the moment when you may have to change course. I mention these challenges right at the outset not to scare you off or to suggest that the journey isn't worth undertaking. Far from it. There is no more thrilling ride, no more worthwhile endeavor. But it can be a frustrating, bitter journey too. Buckle your seat belt and prepare for a lot of hard-won learning.

I've organized the book into nine chapters on the following topics: a writer's work, a writer's education, a writer's craft, a writer's personality, a writer's challenges, a writer's strengths, a writer's relationships, a writer's world, and a writer's career. The chapters contain personal anecdotes, question-and-answer pieces, role plays, multiple choice questions, discussion questions, solicited pieces, exercises, and whatever else I could think of to provide as truthful and helpful a picture of the writing life as I could.

Writers tend to live solitary, even alienated lives. But for a writer to achieve emotional health and to fashion a writing career, relationships are of vital importance. Relationships with editors, agents, and the reading public need to be cultivated. Friendship and intimacy with other human beings also need a writer's attention and cultivation. So I've made a special effort to underline the relational needs of writers and to provide exercises that support relationship-building. There are role plays, discussion questions, and exercises that can be used in writing groups or writers' support groups. There are also exercises meant to help you stretch relationally, whether that stretch is cold-calling an agent or overcoming writers' conference phobia.

A feature of the book are the role play exercises. I use role plays in my psychotherapy practice and creativity consulting work and in many of the workshops I give at writers' conferences. In my writers' conference keynote workshop I have writers volunteer to come up on stage and role play writer-agent and writer-editor interactions. These role plays are always illuminating. The volunteer role players and the audience begin to see how "normal" these interactions are—how straightforward and obvious are the questions, and what obvious, straightforward answers are required—but they also learn how much preparation and personal presence are needed in order for the writer to handle the situation effectively. Guidelines for participating in role plays are given in Chapter 1, page 11, and I do hope that you find a way to try out the examples I've provided throughout the book in a group setting. But even just playing them out in imagination will teach you a lot.

I've also included question-and-answer pieces. Some years back I inaugurated a question-and-answer column for *Callboard Magazine* called

"Staying Sane in the Theater," and I learned from that experience that the question-and-answer format is a resonant one. I hope you'll find these pieces useful. I also solicited personal articles from some people I know. I think that these pieces enrich the book and offer some unusually honest glimpses into the writing life. What is it like to embark on a master's degree in creative writing later in life? What does the psychological relationship between editor and writer feel like from an editor's point of view? These are some of the issues addressed, and I hope you find these anecdotes from working professionals revealing.

If you've been writing for some time you'll recognize the issues I'm presenting in this book and, I hope, you'll find my advice helpful. If you've been dreaming of beginning or are just starting out, this book can serve as a road map, pointing out potholes and forks in the road. No admission ticket is needed to the writing life: entry is absolutely free. You don't need a degree or a license and all your training is on-the-job. But once you enter this Wonderland world, watch out! It will prove a hammering adventure full of mighty sights and knee-buckling descents, magical trances and the occasional migraine headache. Welcome.

1
A Writer's Work

Engineers build bridges so that traffic can get from one side of the river to the other. Their work is to understand how bridges are built. The work of most businesses is manufacturing a product or providing a service and selling that product or service to customers. This is your work if you're employed by General Motors, AT&T, Pepsi-Cola, or McDonalds, and whether you're high up or low down on the corporate totem pole. Most work has to do with simple, everyday things: making a cookie and selling it, making a car and selling it, learning the law and using it, helping people get rid of hernias and cataracts.

Most jobs are simple to explain and understand, even if they are hard to execute. It is easy enough to explain what kind of work personal trainers do, or priests, or politicians. If you're an academic, say, you learn a portion of a field of inquiry, try to add to that body of knowledge, and teach your students about your field. But what exactly is a writer's work? What is a writer's job? What purpose do writers serve and what niche in the ecology of human affairs do they fill? Who pays them for what they do? If the answer to this last question is virtually no one, shouldn't that make us wonder if what they do is wanted or needed?

We have to start at a very basic level to understand what kind of work a writer does and what place that work has in the universe of human affairs. All of these are writers: novelists, poets, playwrights, technical writers, investigative reporters, science writers, columnists, essayists, advertising copywriters, self-help nonfiction writers, history writers, children's book writers, romance writers, mystery writers, television writers, screenwriters. There are also a whole host of others who must write as part of their job descriptions—among them those who write e-mail messages, job-related memos, catalog copy, in-house newsletters, etc. But only some of these are writers in the sense we mean when we say, "I want to be a writer." That is, only some of these people are in their own employ, writing what they want to write. This is the ideal. But what is *this* person's work?

> *"The role of the writer is not to say what we can all say but what we are unable to say."*
>
> —Anais Nin
>
> **Are you ready to articulate what's hard to say but needs saying?**

Consider the following. You're at a party and you meet someone new. Naturally, you ask him what he does.

"I'm a speaker," he replies.

"Oh," you say, furrowing your brow. "What do you speak about?"

"Whatever interests me," he replies. "One day it might be about the dangers of religion. Another day it might be about how the sky looks at twilight."

"Oh. And who pays you to speak?"

"Well, that's tricky. No one, actually. That is, I prepare my speech, then I try to see if someone out there wants to pay me to speak it."

"That could make it hard to pay the bills," you murmur. "Still, that's pretty amazing. You get to just speak about whatever interests you?"

"That's right. I'm a speaker. That's what I do."

"But ..."

"Yes?"

"I'm still a little confused. You just speak your mind?"

"That's it exactly."

"And you really do make a living?"

"Oh, no. Some speakers make millions, but most of us make very little or nothing at all. We don't even get heard. We just prepare our speeches but never get to speak them to an audience. That's what most of us speakers do."

"Let me see if I'm following. You have the perfect freedom to speak your mind, but mostly nobody wants to hear what you have to say and so you live in poverty?"

"That's it! Pretty much."

"Why don't you speak about things people want to hear about?"

"Well, that's an idea. Many speakers do that and many more think about doing that. It's a real question."

"And the answer is?"

"The answer is, if you're lucky enough to want to speak about what people also want to hear about, then it can be a great job—the greatest job on earth. If you're unlucky enough to want to speak about what people don't much want to hear about, then it's very hard to get heard. It's also very hard to try to speak about things you don't want to speak about. It's hard to get your heart and your mind into that kind of speaking. So it's kind of sticky."

"I'd imagine that it's also hard to get the people who might pay you for speaking to even know you exist. That's a sales job, isn't it?"

"How clever of you! A speaker's job is to speak about whatever interests him or her, but it's definitely also a sales job, which many speakers never realize—or, if they realize it, never fully accept."

"So you think your work is important?"

"The most important!"

"Even if you write bad speeches, or good speeches that no one ever gets to hear?"

"Well, no. Not then."

"So—"

"It is the greatest crap shoot on earth. You are staking your whole life on the possibility that the things you want to say will get out there into the ears of your fellow human beings and ignite them, transform them, educate them, amuse them, excite them, alert them, or help them pass a rainy day by the beach. Forgive me for putting it in this blasphemous way, but you are saying, 'I will spend my life being God and creating.' Pretty nice work—but the biggest crap shoot on earth."

"Amazing. Just speaking what you want to speak! It's pretty attractive, the poverty notwithstanding. Could you teach me to be a speaker?"

"There's lots to learn, but there's nothing to teach. Just speak. It's incredibly simple. Just speak. Of course, everyone around you may start to slip away—"

"You know, I'm passionate about pesticides—"

"Then speak!"

"You don't mind?"

"Oh, you want to speak to me? Sorry. I've got to run."

Q & A

I think I want to be a writer, but I don't really know what that means. What kind of life would I get to lead? What does being a writer mean?

Being a writer means relating to life in a certain way. A writer is someone who has to know for herself and do for herself in order to feel alive. She writes stories, poems, novels, essays, or nonfiction books because she has the urge to make meaning. Being a writer means being existential. There are writers who aren't very existential, but as a rule what motivates a person to write is her desire, bordering on a compulsion, to make sense of reality in a personal, idiosyncratic way.

What kind of life is an "existential" life? A precarious one. A nonnormal one. A life of daydreaming and musing. A life of questioning. A life dedicated to putting thoughts down to see what they mean. A life dedicated to big questions, mighty themes, and the essentials of the human condition. You might be writing about two sparrows, but you are asking questions about the meaning of life. You might be writing about the economics of the Pacific Rim, but you are asking big questions about how human beings live, work, interact, and connect. You might be writing about your grandmother, but you are writing about life and death. That is how the existential person spends her day.

Being a writer also means taking on certain special roles in society. The writer leads. The writer is the expert. The writer points an admonishing finger, or a finger that shows the way to something new. The writer makes up the culture's myths and stories. The writer teaches. The writer says: "This is what should be done" and "Here's something you should know." The writer goes on talk shows, is interviewed in the newspaper. The writer is asked for her opinion. The writer tells others what is right and wrong, what is good and bad, what is worthy and unworthy, what is complex and not simple or simple and not complex. When you write something, you are saying, "Listen up!" Writers shout the news and, at their best, tell the most vital truths.

Oh, yes. Being a writer also means writing. This means thinking, mind-traveling, world-building, wordsmithing, creating, manifesting your personality, sitting still, reading and rereading, sweating, typing, daydreaming, discarding, listening, feeling, screaming, loving, hating, erasing, worrying, and lots more. Even writers who love writing hate writing on some days, and even writers who hate writing love writing on some days. Is there more to love than to hate? A writer sits with this painful, perplexing question on her shoulder her whole life as she worries her stories into existence. Whatever the answer, writers write; otherwise they find themselves in the unhappy predicament of being would-be writers, blocked writers, or former writers.

Being a writer also means being a worker. Most writers are unpaid or poorly paid workers. Only a few writers make reasonable amounts of money. Only a very, very few writers make lots of money. You will hear about these very, very few writers the most, because they are celebrities in a celebrity culture and their million-dollar advances and multibook deals are grist for our culture's gossip mill. You will never hear about the writer who wrote a good book and earned $2000 or $4000 from that effort. So our minds are confused on this score. We do not see all the invisible writers; they are not in the papers and not on the talk shows.

But they are everywhere. The numbers of people who are writing, trying to write, or hoping to write are in the millions. The numbers of people who earn a living from writing are only in the thousands. The numbers of people who earn a fortune from writing are in the scores or hundreds. So, unless you are the exception, for you writing will mean making little money; it will mean needing to find money elsewhere; it will mean toiling away under a cloak of invisibility. You will not be considered an expert, because no one will know you. When you shout "Listen up!" few people will listen. You will want to be heard, but you will not get enough of an opportunity.

A writer dreams big; that is the glorious part. A writer needs to do the hard work of writing and the hard work of acquiring an audience. Those parts breed frustration and disappointment. So the writing life is a mixed bag. This is what it means to be a writer: all this dark and all this light.

THE HARD WORK OF NOT WRITING

In 1974 I spent a few months in Iceland, at the other end of the island from Reykjavik, and then flew on to London. I stayed in a flat in Hampstead, in the north of London just off the Finchley Road, that was owned by a woman I'd met while in school at the University of Oregon. She was renting out two of the three bedrooms to two fellows and the third bedroom, her own, which was empty while she remained in Oregon, was to be mine for a month or two. I got there on a beautiful June day, dressed in a purple parka I'd bought to wear in Iceland (where it had snowed at Easter), and met my flat mates.

These were two educated fellows with very different attitudes and lives. One, whose actual job I no longer remember, accompanied singers on the piano and lived for music. The other, an advertising man, had a hyphenated last name and a personality to match. I hung out with the accompanist. One evening he wandered into my room and caught me writing. At that time I was writing some scenes set in Budapest for a World War II novel. The scenes were based on a story that a Hungarian friend of mine had told me about the time his life had been spared by a young German soldier during the Nazi occupation of Hungary. I was writing the scenes badly—but I was writing them.

> *"Nobody can become perfect by merely ceasing to act."*
> —Bhagavad-gita
>
> **Are you writing perfect books by not writing?**

Michael watched me from the doorway while I jotted down a last thought. When I put my pen down, he said, "You actually write. My brother calls himself a writer, but he never writes." A small thing to remember, but I remember it clearly. Nowadays, when I counsel blocked writers, I return, as every blocked writer himself or herself does, to that simple observation. What distinguishes writers from nonwriters and would-be writers is that writers write.

But the blocked writer is working phenomenally hard. For the person who wants to write, not writing is terribly arduous work. As Fran Lebowitz remarked, "Not writing is a big effort. When I started getting real work done, I realized how much easier it is to write than not to write. Not writing is probably the most exhausting profession I've ever encountered. It's very physically wearing not to write—I mean, if you're supposed to be writing."

Every blocked writer knows this, every blocked painter knows this, every blocked songwriter knows this. Every actor who has stopped auditioning knows this. Every potter avoiding her wheel knows this. Every singer not singing knows this. Not doing the work you want to do takes long hours—even long years—and tremendous effort.

The philosopher Immanuel Kant made a distinction between blameworthiness and praiseworthiness which to my mind remains interesting to this day. He awarded moral points not for the action itself, but according to whether a person found it hard or easy to do that good thing. If, say, you found it easy not to covet your neighbor's wife and so you didn't covet her, no praise. But if you found it terribly hard, if it drove you half-crazy, if lust and nothing but lust occupied all your waking thoughts, but somehow you freed yourself from your obsession and didn't act on your feelings, that, Kant argued, deserved some real praise.

So if you find it easy to write and you write, congratulations. But don't ask for praise. If, however, you find it hard to write, if fears and doubts have you blocked, if uncertainties and anxieties of all kinds get in your way, and still you manage to write, in some ledger book somewhere you are racking up points. You can be sure of it!

Remember: not writing is real work. It is as real as writing, and much less satisfying.

ROLE PLAY

In each chapter you'll be provided with a role play exercise. There are several ways to use these exercises.

* The first is in a group setting. You and another person enact the role play while the rest of the group members observe the interaction. Then you all join in a general discussion, the role players going first and describing their reactions to the experience. If you're using the role play this way, have a group member who isn't part of the role play copy out the instructions, so that neither partner sees the other's instructions.

* A second way to use these role plays is with a partner, where the two of you enact the role play and then discuss the interaction just between yourselves. In this case, copy out your own instructions and

try not to read your partner's. When you've played out the situation as many times as you want, varying your responses and trying out different strategies, take time to debrief and discuss what you learned.

✳ The third way to use these role plays is for you to play both roles yourself, a variation of a gestalt therapy technique called "empty chair" work (because when you are addressing the other person you are talking to an empty chair). In this case, set up two chairs facing each other and switch from chair to chair, actively dialoguing as you alternate roles. This is a very powerful and useful technique, because the task of strongly adopting one position and then quickly letting go of it for another teaches us a lot about how to detach and free ourselves from "cherished ideas" that may not be serving us well.

✳ A fourth way to make use of these role plays is to play them out in imagination. Imagine the situation presented, get into the skin of each character, actively dialogue, and then process your thoughts and feelings by writing several paragraphs on the experience. Focus especially on what you learned and on any new behaviors you might want to adopt as a consequence of what you learned.

The following are some guidelines for enacting role plays:

1. Take time to carefully read the description of your role (or both roles, if you are working alone). Get a sense of the text and the subtext. What's being demanded of you? What's the issue? What are you supposed to reveal and what are you supposed to keep secret? What is the desired outcome? Do you have a sense of who you are and what you want? Don't begin the role play until you feel ready.

2. Spontaneously create a detailed character with a past, a present, and a future whose pain and pleasure you feel, whose motivations you understand, and whose idiosyncratic quirks you manifest. If you are playing a writer in the role play you may want to play yourself, but you may also want to play someone who is bolder than you—or more direct, or a better salesperson—to see what it feels like to wear a different skin. If you are playing an agent or an editor, try to imagine who they really are and what they really do.

3. Choose a set-up. You might choose to enact a formal face-to-face meeting, a phone conversation, a scheduled fifteen-minute meeting at a writers' conference, an informal encounter at a party. Try the same role play using different set-ups. "Cold calls" make for especially valuable learning experiences and should be included whenever possible.

4. Be creative and flexible. The details of the situation are yours to create. Even if the role play sets the two of you up as antagonists, a certain level of cooperation is needed. If the person opposite you is playing an editor and she tells you that she can't buy your novel but that she happens to be looking for self-help nonfiction at the moment, decide on the spot whether you want to explore that avenue (and maybe become a self-help nonfiction writer just like that!) or pass. Real life situations can provide you with exactly these challenges and opportunities, and you want to be able to handle them flexibly and creatively.

5. Even though you are cooperating to make the role play work, still be adamant. If your role demands that you act rushed (as most literary agents and editors are rushed), maintain that energy unless the person across from you does a good job of slowing you down, say by interesting you in her manuscript. If you are trying to find something out from the other person, be persistent until all hope of doing so is lost. One of the goals of role playing is to "hold your intention" even if the other person makes your job extremely difficult.

6. Do not stop the role play because you feel stuck, uncertain, blocked, upset, anxious, or frustrated. These are exactly the sorts of things you can expect to happen in real life, and experiencing them in the role play, working them through, and later thinking about them are vital parts of the exercise.

7. When you are done with the role play, take time to discuss the experience. Make use of the questions provided at the end of each role play and invent additional questions of your own.

ROLE PLAY:
Learning to Talk About Your Work

Person A: You are a writer. You recently applied for a residency at a writers' retreat. Now you've been asked to come in for an individual interview to explain "the nature of your work." No further information about what's wanted from you is available. The day has arrived. Are you ready to discuss "the nature of your work"? What do you mean to say? What would you like to emphasize?

Person B: You are the director of a writers' retreat and are interviewing writers for the last available spot. You mean to give it to the writer who can most concretely and compellingly explain "the nature of his or her work."

You are tired of the vague, inarticulate responses you usually get and feel particularly irritable today. You mean to interrupt the writer if you are not getting a clear picture of the genre the writer works in, the sorts of situations, themes, or characters the writer investigates, the psychological, philosophical, artistic, or just plain human significance of the work, or whatever other information it takes for you to really understand and appraise "the nature of the writer's work."

(Also enact this as a phone conversation.)

Debriefing Questions

Questions for the writer to answer:

1. What did the experience feel like?
2. How did it feel to be examined and "pushed" in this manner?
3. In describing "the nature of your work," what might you now include or exclude?
4. What did you learn about the task of describing your work to another person?
5. What else did you learn about yourself, your work, or the experience of being interviewed about your work?

Questions for the writers' retreat director to answer:

1. What was the experience like?
2. Did you like or dislike your role?
3. What worked for you in the writer's presentation? What impressed you?
4. What didn't work for you in the writer's presentation? What irritated, bored, or confused you?
5. What did you learn about what you yourself need to do in order to be able to articulate "the nature of your work"?

Questions for the observers to answer:

1. What especially struck you about the interaction?
2. Did you get a clear picture of the writer's work?
3. Did you feel yourself "siding" with the retreat director or with the writer?
4. What seemed to work in the writer's presentation? What seemed not to work?
5. What appears to be called for at such times? What might you include in your own presentation to help communicate the nature of your work as a writer to others?

THE HARD WORK OF STARTING

Donna Levin is the author of two novels, *Extraordinary Means* and *California Street*, and two books about writing, *Get That Novel Started* and *Get That Novel Written*. She provided the following observations.

On Starting Again (and Again and Again)

Everything about writing is hard (hard? boy, is that an understatement; why don't we just acknowledge that it's torture on a good day), but starting is the bloody worst.

When I was twenty-seven, my father bought me a word processor (a giant thing with eight-and-a-half-inch floppies and no hard drive; you'd laugh at it now, but it was state of the art then). I had to learn to use it, so I had to type something, and from typing there's only a very short hop to what you can call writing, even if you have to be generous to do so.

My father's gift was what finally pried my fingers off the edge of the cliff I had been holding onto. I had wanted to be a writer all my life. But although the difference between typing and writing is small, the difference between thinking about writing and actually writing is great.

Before I was a writer, when I was just a wannabe, my own books were perfect: Well-reviewed and widely read, they could move you to tears and make you laugh out loud. The only thing wrong with my books was that they weren't written yet.

I was well aware that once I started writing I would have to give up the notion of being perfect. In spite of this enlightened state, I had waited many years to start. In my late twenties the dream began to deplete itself; still, I needed that push. Many things besides my father's IBM encouraged me to start, but the IBM it was, and for that I'm grateful.

> "To write is to write is to write is to write is to write is to write is to write is to write."
>
> —Gertrude Stein
>
> **Are you writing?**

Over the course of the next three years, I wrestled a first novel down onto paper. I sent it out, and began accumulating rejections. With each one I felt as though my self-esteem had been placed quivering on a cutting board and then smashed with a hammer. It was confirmation of my worst fear: that I wasn't really a writer.

I no longer see "not publishing"—and certainly not each rejection— as the same line between being and nothingness, but it was in this unchipper frame of mind that I sat down to start my second novel. I'd had an idea for another book for awhile; I'd even written a rough draft of the first chapter when I got stuck on the final rewrite of the first novel. Yet starting this new book was equally hard, for different reasons. I had long abandoned the fantasies of effortless success. I knew that I was good at dialogue and weak in plot. But now I had growing evidence that whatever I was good at, I wasn't good enough. Each morning as I dragged myself to the IBM my father had given me, holding my coffee-mixed-with-hot-chocolate, I heard the gods laugh.

I never did sell that first, first novel. But I did sell the second novel which, by sleight of publishing hand, became my first.

In the midst of the ecstasy of selling a book, I congratulated myself that the agony was over. Never again would I have to dig so deep into myself to tap into the well of faith and ambition. Never again would starting be so difficult.

And, to quote Dorothy Parker, I am Marie of Rumania.

With the second-written, first-published, novel coming down the pike, I had to start the third-written, second-published. I was surprised by the problems: I was stuck on the plot; feared I was running out of material; couldn't find the right tone. It didn't help that my writing group hated my early chapters.

Gradually the book did begin to come together. And I sold that one, too, though only after what seemed like a lot of effort. I didn't know what effort was. I found out more about effort when the next novel I wrote did not sell, even though I believed (and still do) that it was my most accomplished so far.

And here's where the paradigm shift comes in. At each previous point I had suffered a crisis, yet at the end I had thought that at least I had learned something incontrovertible: That you get better as you write, that persistence is rewarded. Something like that.

In fact, all I learned was that there's little to learn. That there are no rules about the marketplace, or about the trajectory of one's career. That there's no equation between time spent and money earned, or fame acquired. That in fact you really never do know whether you're "good" or not. Consider this: most of the books on the bestseller list today will be forgotten in another decade, and while some will survive, even the most gifted critics would have trouble predicting which ones.

I had to start yet yet yet again. I don't even know how I did. There's no logic to it. But then, there's no logic to writing, either.

Somewhere in the midst of all this I wrote a book called Get That Novel Started. *My dream? To be to a few others what the IBM was to me.*

Sanctifying In-Dwelling

A writer's first job is to sanctify in-dwelling. By this I mean that a writer needs to say to herself clearly, forcefully, and even out loud, "There is value in my being alone with my own brain. I will make time and space for my own thoughts, even if that scares me to death." Solitude may badly scare her because, alone with her thoughts, she is likely to come up against her fears, doubts, and disparaging self-talk. She may begin to feel sad, angry, discouraged, and agitated. But despite these real difficulties, in-dwelling must be sanctified: writers must commit to living with their own thoughts.

In order to sanctify in-dwelling a writer needs to clean her mental house of bad mental habits, habits that produce anxiety, fog, and a desire to flee. All the meditative philosophies ask their students to do this and they rightly call what they demand "practice." Writers need to practice conscious, committed in-dwelling. The writer builds a bubble—a sanctified bubble, a church of consciousness, a sacred mental space—which she enters with the intention of boldly, bravely, and unflinchingly communicating with herself. She is about to have an important chat with herself. She is about to create.

To combat these unfortunate mental habits, a writer should:

1. Think of himself/herself as a god or a goddess, not as a bug.
2. Call himself/herself no bad names.
3. Calm down and let the world stop.
4. Make no odious comparisons with writers who have it better, have published more, look as though they're more talented, etc.
5. Activate his/her brain, freeing neurons by the billions in the service of deepened consciousness.
6. Stay in the present, neither reliving past failures nor fine-tuning a future Nobel Prize acceptance speech.
7. Love himself/herself.
8. Let in mystery.
9. Focus on ideas and on his/her work, not on himself/herself.

Good writing follows good thinking. Good thinking requires a patch of quiet. What a writer needs more than anything else is silence, a silence emptied of the incessant chattiness that goes on in the typical mind. Learn to grow silent. Don't be afraid. Yes, you'll encounter some frights and difficulties. But then the writing will come.

To recapitulate, then:

1. Call solitude precious. Sanctify in-dwelling.
2. Make it precious and useful through practice.

Q & A

How many hours a day do writers write?

Typically, not so many. Some writers manage to write eight hours a day, but many writers would consider a three-hour writing stint quite a successful writing day.

Think of it this way. When you're actually writing, it's not hard to write a page or two an hour. In three hours you'd have an average of four or five pages done. That would amount to three books a year (do the math). Few writers produce this much. Even if you factor in revising and calculate that for every hour of writing an hour of revising will eventually be needed, then your three hours a day still turns into a book or two a year. Not many writers produce this much, either. Even if you throw in some research time, days off for vacation, days off because you hate the work and just can't stand to look at it, and so on, three hours a day on most days would probably translate into one book a year, which is a higher rate of productivity than most writers ever muster. That would amount to forty or fifty books completed in a writing life. How many writers manage that?

When we hear that a writer has written forty books, we think that's an amazing feat and even something of a conjuring trick. Not only is that person brilliant but he or she must come from Jupiter and have sold his or her soul to the Muse. Yet it's entirely likely that a "prolific" writer of this sort is only writing three hours a day, two days out of three. That's about all the magic that's involved.

> *"I try to work every day, even when I'm not motivated. Ritual is very important to me."*
>
> —Mel Ramos
>
> **Are you good at ritual, routine, and regularity?**

So don't let it worry you if you hear that some writer writes twelve hours a day and you don't. Don't let it worry you if you hear that some writer turns out fifteen or twenty pages of prose a day. Don't let it worry you (or make you too envious) that the writer down the block has a legacy and gets to sit home all day writing, while you don't. Just determine to write two or three hours a day, two days out of three. The next time you look up, twenty or thirty books will be finished.

MAKING CHOICES

No agent has been willing to give your screenplay a reading. Most don't answer your query letter; the majority of the rest reply with a form letter refusing to see it. The few who ask to see it don't respond. Finally you manage to get in touch with an agent to whom you sent your screenplay. It turns out that he's actually glanced at it. But he tells you he never bothered to read it because he could tell from that glance that it's strictly amateurish: it goes on for more than a hundred twenty pages, the main character doesn't appear on the first page, and the characters sometimes speak for more than two sentences in a row (do you think you're writing Shakespeare?). In response, do you:

    (a) Bring to his attention all the famous screenplays that violate his so-called rules?

    (b) Hire a hit man to kill him?

    (c) Cry hard, then leave the business?

    (d) Laugh, shake your head, then leave the business?

    (e) Recommit to screenwriting but rethink your strategy?

You might think that I mean to suggest (e). But your answer depends on how you define your work as a writer. If your desire is to entertain thirteen-year-old boys (which means men of my age, too, who still need Terminators and things exploding), or if the movies so matter to you that you feel obliged to write screenplays rather than books, or if you feel compelled, because of karma and predestination, to live and die in Los Angeles, attending meetings, dropping names, getting optioned, and seeing and being seen, then you will want to take this agent's advice to heart. His message is simple: you ain't nobody, kid, at least in terms of Hollywood. And to learn how to become a Hollywood somebody, you need to learn how to follow the rules you need to follow, break the rules you need to break, and network and party in the appropriate fashion with people in Hollywood who are already somebodies. Above all you must live, breathe, and understand the reality—not the fantasy—of movies and the movie industry.

However, (d) may be your answer. You may want to laugh and take an early exit, recommitting yourself not to screenwriting within the Hollywood studio system but to your need to lead, speak some truths, create subtle worlds, and all those "higher" needs that drive writers. This may involve staying in film but as a full-fledged independent filmmaker, doing everything yourself and by doing everything getting the chance to make the movies that are in your heart to make. It may involve deciding to write novels, which have no greater guarantee than screenplays of being wanted but which, when they are wanted, at least are more likely to remain in their original shape and not become the hybrid creation of a studio and its rewriters. Or you may decide to write "creative" nonfiction, nonfiction that allows you to speak in your own voice and detail angles of the universe. In short, in terms of screenwriting. this agent has thrown cold water in your face. Shocked, but refreshed, you get to decide all over again what your ambitions and needs really are.

Q & A

Why do writers write?

To save the species and to light the way for others. At its most important, writing is *the* ethical, existential occupation par excellence. But there are lots of other ways to conceptualize the writer's job, ones that are more modest than making it into a holy kind of thing. You may want to entertain. You may want to learn something new by writing about it. You may want to communicate something interesting or amusing to others. You may want to make a buck from your accumulated knowledge and experience. You may want to create and inhabit an imaginary world. You may just want to better organize your own universe. Consider the following from Ed Hooks, an actor, acting teacher, and writer:

> *"Technique alone is never enough. You have to have passion. Technique alone is just an embroidered pot holder."*
> —Raymond Chandler
>
> **Have you got the passion?**

> The Ultimate Scene and Monologue Sourcebook *happened because I could no longer keep a growing volume of scenes, plays and monologues in my head. My acting students would ask for scene suggestions, and I would search my memory like a computer doing a "find file" routine. But after you have seen actors present many hundreds of scenes, and after you have read a thousand plays or more, and after you have sat in the audience at hundreds of plays all across the country, you get to a place where things start running together in your brain.*
>
> *You begin to get situations from one of Neil Simon's many plays mixed up with similar situations in plays by Alan Ayckbourn. One day you realize that all you can remember about Chekhov's "The Cherry Orchard" is that it is a play about Russia. So* The Ultimate Scene and Monologue Sourcebook *was my way of organizing myself, of putting in writing what I was having trouble keeping in memory. The book was a service to me personally, as well as a guide for my acting students and actors everywhere. It began with my class*

> *notebooks and expanded into the advertised "Guide to Over 1,000*
> *Monologues and Scenes from More than 300 Contemporary Plays"*
> *only after I had entered into publication discussions. It started out*
> *with just a simple, pressing need to get myself organized."*

Your reasons for writing may be modest or grand. Whatever they are, I bet you have some. Don't you have the itch? Don't you have your reasons? Then write!

FOOD FOR THOUGHT

"The nobility of a writer's calling will always be rooted in
two commitments difficult to observe: refusal to lie about
what we know, and resistance to oppression."—Albert Camus

Are you committed to telling important truths? Does it matter if the struggles to get them down and to get them heard are fierce ones?

"The artist is responsible for the music he performs."—Pablo Casals

Do you take responsibility for what you write? Is "taking responsibility" one of your primary jobs?

Books through the ages have earned humanity's
high regard as semi-sacred objects."—Richard Kluger

Are you doing sacred work or profane work? What do these distinctions mean?

"Painting for me is a freedom attained, constantly consolidated, vigilantly guarded so as to draw from it the power to paint more."—Alberto Burri

Is writing a declaration of freedom? Have you declared that freedom for yourself?

"A truly creative musician is capable of producing, from his own imagination, melodies that are more authentic than folklore itself."—Hector Villa-Lobos

What is authentic writing? Is that what you're aiming for?

"I love all men who dive. Any fish can swim near the surface, but it takes a great whale to go downstairs five miles or more."—Herman Melville

Do you love to go deep? Are you willing to dive, explore, and bring back treasures?

"What shall I sing? What shall I paint? What shall I perform?
I paint the real situation, to make people aware of what is going on and what are the deepest roots of our illness."—Thich Nhat Hanh

Is this how you define your work: to fathom the roots of our illness?

"Listen carefully to first criticisms of your work. Note just what it is about the work that the critics don't like—then cultivate it. That's the part of your work that's individual and worth keeping."—Jean Cocteau
What is individuality? Are you cultivating yours?

"The writer has taken unto himself the former function of the priest or prophet. He presumes to order and legislate the people's life. There is no person more arrogant than the writer."—Cornelius Register
Are you arrogant enough to lead and legislate?

"I just hear a sound coming into my head and hope to catch it with my hands."—Erroll Garner
Are you good at catching your own writing thoughts?

"I read the play as many times as I can. I also sleep on it: I literally put it under my pillow."—Elizabeth Franz
Do you keep your writing close enough?

"If what I write makes a woman in the Canadian mountains cry and she writes and tells me about it, especially if she says 'I read it to Tom when he came in from work and he cried too,' I feel I have succeeded."—Kathleen Norris
How do you want your readers to react? What kind of impression are you trying to make?

"To live in the world of creation—to get into it and stay in it— to frequent it and haunt it—to think intensely and fruitfully— to woo combinations and inspirations into being by a depth and continuity of attention and meditation—this is the only thing."—Henry James
How often do you live in the world of creation? Only rarely? Sometimes? Or around the clock?

"When one likes something passionately, the rest is excluded from consideration, naturally. The more the means are limited, the stronger the expression: that, perhaps, explains the choice of a limited palette."—Pierre Soulages
Are you writing with a limited palette? Is that necessary and is that unfortunate?

"Hard days, lots of work, no money, too much silence. Nobody's fault. You chose it."—Bill Barich
Have you committed to the life as well as the work?

2 A Writer's Education

If a writer's work is essentially to write what's on her mind and to write it well, what education does she require?

The short answer is, none in particular. Any training she gets in good thinking, all her life experiences, and any reading she does will each prove useful. But, as with speech, which only requires a language and a speaker willing to speak, all being a writer needs is a written language and a desire to write. The education comes as the writer lives and as she writes. There is very little for her to learn about writing in the abstract: she must try her hand at it, make her own mistakes, learn the craft from the inside out, and learn by doing.

> *"Training to be a writer is a slow and continuous process, with time off for human behavior."*
> —Marie-Elise
>
> **Are you writing enough to allow for slow, continuous learning?**

Learning by doing is especially important. There is more to be learned from writing a bad novel than from attending twenty good novel-writing workshops. There's a fantastic amount to be learned from writing two bad novels and then a good one. And to do that writing, a writer needs inner permission to write. Sometimes that permission isn't there automatically. Just as a child in a certain kind of mean-spirited household needs permission to speak, sometimes authors withhold permission to write from themselves. So part of a writer's self-education may be learning why she withholds that permission in order to give it to herself.

The writer also needs life experiences. It is certainly possible to write a fine novel at twenty, but it is also the case that one knows a lot more at thirty, forty, fifty, sixty, and so on. That increased knowledge gives the writer a better chance to write the novel that was always in her heart to write. Gaining experience is not the same as living recklessly, nor is it something that one sets out to acquire, as one sets out to acquire skins and trophy horns on a big-game hunt. But the basic experiences of life—loving, raising a child, crying hard as an adult, being fired, and all the rest—do improve one's writing as nothing else can.

Then the writer needs to educate herself about the marketplace. Here workshops, panel discussions, classes, and the like may prove useful. It is good to hear agents, editors, and published authors talk about what they think is publishable. The writers and would-be writers in the audience may disagree with what they hear. They may want the facts to be otherwise, hate the "bottom line" attitudes they hear espoused, and resent the long odds against them. They may even find themselves unable to hear what's being said, so anxious does the subject make them. But if they want to become writers who sell regularly and sustain a career, they have no choice but to learn the lessons of the marketplace.

So the recipe is simple enough. Feel like you can write. Write. Live. Learn about the marketplace. That's about it.

THE CRUCIBLE OF CHILDHOOD

The first education we get is in the crucible of childhood. What happens there forms us, marks us, haunts us, even hounds us. It is vital to remember that at some point in our life—at many different points, really—we have the job of stepping back and determining if our current path is to our liking and whether we are still playing out the dramas and still lugging around the baggage of childhood.

What are real childhoods like? What do we learn in the crucible of childhood and what must we unlearn? How are we helped to become our best selves by our parents and by our culture and how are we hindered? Each writer and would-be writer has his or her own story, some darker than others, some more disastrous. But each one is complex, pivotal, provocative, and real. Consider the following thumb-nail sketches provided by four different writers.

Jane described her childhood as follows:

> I was raised by my grandmother. My father, who didn't want a daughter, left, and my mother was physically and emotionally abusive. My relationship with my mother was like having a jealous older sister.
>
> At about age three I was molested by my grandfather. When I was about five I was enrolled in dance. My grandmother would take me. I loved it and felt I excelled at it but my grandmother didn't consider it a stable endeavor and my mother appeared disappointed that I wasn't good enough.
>
> I stopped dancing for two years, returned, and continued dancing out of my own desire to regain the happiness I once experienced. I didn't meet my father until I was ten. I admired his musical ability and wanted him to see that ability in me, so as to have a connection with him. But what was fostered most in me was the idea that I was not talented enough, not pretty, and, of course, stupid.

> "When I was a ten-year-old bookworm and used to kiss the dust jacket pictures of authors as if they were icons, it used to amaze me that these remote people could provoke me to love."
>
> —Erica Jong
>
> **Which writers have you loved? What does that love signify?**

According to Tom:

My childhood was turbulent. My mother married four times and committed suicide in her late fifties. We moved all around the South a lot because my natural father was a hospital administrator. I went to sixteen different schools before graduating from high school. Mother had six kids, three of whom died at birth. My natural father was a horror, evidently an abusive man, but I can't remember him in any detail. He left when I was ten, at which time I stopped having fainting spells and bad headaches.

Mother remarried a sweet, ineffectual man when I was thirteen. She was forever confiding in me, quite inappropriately, her sexual frustrations with him. Evidently, he was impotent. She divorced him after a few years and subsequently married two more men, one an alcoholic and the last a nice man who soon died from Parkinson's Disease. Tennessee Williams couldn't have written a better scenario than my childhood.

Anne described growing up in Germany as the child of one Jewish and one gentile parent:

My father was a psychiatrist and my mother a psychologist who specialized in family relationships. There was constant friction between them and they divorced when I was twenty-three. Before that, when the war began, my father was protected from being sent to a concentration camp by being married to a gentile, and he became terribly dependent on my mother's good will. But still there was constant fighting and accusations and each parent tried to use me as a pawn in their power struggle.

My mother was the dominant personality—she had seen my father through medical school and never let him forget what he owed her. It was she who found tutors and other activities for me when a new law terminated school attendance for all Mischlinge (children of Jewish-gentile parentage) in 1942. It was my mother who arranged after the war for us to emigrate to America.

Both my parents were success-oriented. My mother was a very powerful person who seemed to be able to do things other people would find impossible even to try, like getting my father out of a Gestapo jail after he was arrested for helping some Jewish patients commit suicide to avoid transportation to Auschwitz. I always felt I had to compete, too, to be better than other kids

at what I did, get better grades, live up to higher standards. But I knew
that in order to break away I had to do it in an area in which neither of my
parents was competent. That's one of the main reasons I went into fiction.

Angela, who became a playwright after starting out as an actress, described her childhood in the following way:

My childhood was traumatic and full of upheaval—although it felt quite
normal to me, of course. I was adopted at a very early age by my parents
who, after having one son, could no longer have children. My father was
a minister, my mother a painter and model. When I was age three my father
left the ministry and my parents divorced and married the parents of my best
friend (my mother married her father and my father married her mother).

My stepfather was a psychiatrist and although extremely successful
in his practice he was a very disturbed man and the brunt of it was placed
on me. My father became an alcoholic meanwhile and although the families
stayed in contact, because of the relationships involved, he was quite non-
present for twenty years. I was raped at the age of twelve and became
severely anorexic after that. I was always very emotional and moody and
my mother and stepfather would call me Sarah Bernhardt and encourage
my performing. Everybody always thought that I was very smart but
very screwed up and that the theater was the best place for me to be.

Not all childhoods are as dramatic and traumatic as these. But they all provide us with our first education. Some of what we learn props us up and supports us; some of it just about ruins us. Whatever we learn, we're bound to encounter it again in our writing.

Q & A

Where do you learn how to write?

In front of a blank piece of paper or a blank computer screen.

I think you can learn some things from classes and workshops. I give workshops, so I hope I'm providing participants with something of value. You can certainly learn something from editors, who as a rule have a knack for helping writers write more leanly and clearly. You can learn things from your readers, the kind and the critical alike, from books on writing, from articles in writing magazines. But all of that is secondary. You learn about writing by faithfully writing, faithfully reading what you've written, and faithfully revising. You learn by writing whole books that are terrible. You learn from your own mistakes. You learn from your own successes. You learn by writing.

Period.

ON FORMAL EDUCATION

Jan Johnson Drantell, former managing editor at Harper San Francisco, free-lance writer and editor, and author (with Leslie Simon) of *A Music I No Longer Heard: The Early Death of a Parent* (Simon and Schuster, 1998), provided the following observations on getting an MFA in creative writing.

> *"There are critical years after school when you are trying to find out what you want to do with your work."*
> —Robert Bechtle
>
> **You've got your degree. Now what?**

Happy Birthday to Me:
Or a Brief Treatise on Earning
an MFA in My Fiftieth Year

I've been writing since I taught myself how to use my father's manual typewriter and carbon paper to make a neighborhood newspaper the summer I was seven or eight. In 1972 (at age twenty-four), I began my editing career. I shifted from a corporate publishing job to free-lance editing in 1990, chiefly because, although I was good at management, budgets, supervision, etc., I was tired of them. I wanted to get back to my first love—working with a writer to make his or her manuscript the best it could be. (I work primarily with non-fiction books, in the areas of spirituality, self-help, creativity, new thought, and I do heavy, rewrite editing.) In 1994, I decided to get that MFA I'd wanted in my twenties.

When I first began talking about going back to school, I'd been working at home for four years. My daughter had graduated from high school and taken off for college on the East Coast. I wanted community, I said, a group of peers to hang out with. I wanted to give myself time and space to write. Fine, all fine, my friends said, especially those who already had advanced degrees. But why the degree? You're already established as an editor, beginning to be established as a writer. You'll know as much as—or more than—most of your teachers. It boiled down to this: outside validation, the security and status of letters. I wanted them.

Fast-forward three years: I did find community of sorts. I belong to two ongoing writers' groups as a direct result of taking the degree. I learned new skills. I experimented with different voices, different styles. My writing improved. Unlike many of my younger peers, I didn't find a mentor among the faculty, but I wasn't exactly looking for one. Given that I come from the "question authority" generation, I struggled sometimes

*with not being recognized by some of the faculty for being their peer
in experience and publishing. (On the other hand, I could recount specific
things I learned from each of them.) I found time and space to write.
My sense of purpose and discipline as a writer intensified.*

*Was it "worth it" to get the degree? Yes, and no. Near as I can tell, six
months from my vantage point as a newly minted MFA, I'm going to keep
doing pretty much what I've been doing for the last seven years. But a
woman I've edited for seven years says I'm better at it now. Diversifying
my own writing repertoire and practice has made me a better editor. I'm
also writing more: short fiction, poetry, non-fiction. I've published one
story already, and had an essay accepted for a book on Muriel Rukeyser.
I'm more creative about thinking about new writing projects for myself.
I'm currently working on two non-fiction book proposals, plus a new draft
of the novel I did for my thesis. Am I going to "use" the degree for its
ostensible purpose as a teaching degree? Although I've applied for one job
(and been turned down even before the interview stage), right now I tend
to think not. For me, writing is what the degree was about, and what my
days are about. I enjoy the "teaching" aspects of my editing work—helping
writers see what's working and what's not, teaching them stylistic and
organizational skills. But tenure track, full-time teaching jobs are scarce
and, quite frankly, I can make more money editing than I could teaching.*

*But, hey, I've got the letters. And although it goes against my Minnesota-
reticence grain to say so, I'm proud of myself for earning them.*

MAKING CHOICES

You would like to write a novel, but you don't have an idea for a novel.
Do you:

    (a) Attend a "Find that novel idea!" workshop?

    (b) Take a creative writing class?

    (c) Join a writing group?

    (d) Sit in front of the computer screen until some words come?

    (e) Open yourself up to a novel idea?

The best answer is (e). The best way to come up with an idea for a novel
is to open yourself up to your own thoughts and feelings.

This is not the same as walking around muttering, "What am I thinking?
What am I feeling?" or "What shall I write? What shall I write?" To receive an
idea for a novel, you simply treat life as if it matters and furrow your brow at
everything you don't understand. In a corner of awareness, you are saying

> "Not knowing when
> the dawn will come,
> I open every door."
>
> —Emily Dickinson
>
> **Where does your
> education come from?
> Is every door
> open to let it in?**

things like, "Why in God's name did that girl do that? What could she have been thinking?" You hold onto questions like that, turning them over wordlessly, activating your curiosity and your imagination, until, all of a sudden, a girl in a white dress wanders into a ramshackle house in an Arkansas town and your novel begins.

You *could* just sit at the computer screen. Something would probably come. You could also join a writing group since writing groups can be helpful. Or you could take a class or workshop; sometimes creative writing classes and workshops are useful. But there is no substitute for holding onto the intention to write, opening yourself up to writing ideas, and rushing to the computer when an idea strikes. An idea for a novel is just an idea, and to have ideas you need a brain that is activated and functioning. Turn on all the switches; throw open all the windows.

EDUCATING YOURSELF
ABOUT YOUR OWN WRITING

Many people who want to write don't manage to write. But all people who do manage to write still get blocked sometimes. Part of a writer's education is learning how to handle blocks that arise when a current piece is stalled and has its problems. The solution to the problem in every case would seem to be the same: read what you've written, see what's wrong, and make the necessary changes. Indeed, this *is* the answer. But all too often it's just very hard to "see" what's wrong with one's writing.

Because we've made an investment in the piece, because we've traveled down one road and don't really feel like beginning again and starting down another, because we stubbornly cling to the hope that the piece is really all right and that nobody will notice its flaws—for these and all kinds of similar psychological and practical reasons, we turn a blind eye toward the work. We *look* like we're rereading, but in fact the work is swimming before our eyes, out of focus and completely unanalyzable.

Take the following example from my creativity consulting practice.

A well-known short story writer came in wanting help unblocking. She'd worked on a first novel pretty steadily for two years running, then blocked. She hadn't been able to approach the novel all spring; and while she experienced not working as painful and distressing, she couldn't find her way back into it.

To my ear, the following seemed true. First, she seemed to be "a real writer." I might have inferred this from the fact that her stories had won prizes and been anthologized and that she taught short story writing at the university level. But primarily I knew this by the way she used language, talked about her writing, and "went inside" to answer my questions. This was not a would-be writer but a writer, which meant that I would not need to do a certain kind of identity work, offer certain kinds of encouragement, or dispute certain kinds of negative self-talk.

Second, I did not get the sense that she felt the writing of a novel was something "too big" for her to do. I sensed that she felt entitled to write novels and equal to writing novels: she just couldn't write this novel. However, because she'd started out writing short stories and had persisted in that sort of writing for many years, this issue was still a question mark. Often writers choose projects of a simple scale, complexity, or perceived difficulty because they don't feel equal to the task of writing something longer or more complex. Of course, the reasons behind such a choice don't always involve self-esteem: they can also be about temperament and outlook. But if you regularly choose "small" work rather than "large" work, it's important to know the reasons why, especially if you're having problems with a larger work.

It also seemed to me that her life was neither too chaotic nor too unbalanced to account for the blockage. She was in an intimate relationship about which she had no pressing complaints. She lived by teaching writing and didn't have to work a disturbing day job. She didn't disparage her abilities or provoke me to inquire about depression, anxiety, or an addiction. No conflicts were apparent and no traumas were reported. As to personality traits, I sensed no particular excesses or insufficiencies. Nor did I sense that she was creating reasons not to write, avoiding the responsibilities of freedom, or somehow in a wrong self-relationship.

Moment by moment, I ruled out avenues to investigate. Finally, I concluded that the problem was less "in her" and much more "about the work"—that is, that it probably had something to do with the way this precise

> *"The only sound advice I can give to the young writer is to tell him to have faith in himself."*
>
> —Howard Fast

Do you have faith in your ability to write, publish, and live the writer's life? If not, how will you acquire it?

novel was not working and something to do with the fact that, since it was her first novel, she was not able to recognize what about the work was stymying her. So I had her tell me about the novel.

She did, and I listened. I was not listening for what the novel told me about her, although of course it was revealing in that way. I was listening to hear what about it still seemed meaningful to her and where, conversely, it seemed tangled or dead. As it turned out, the novel was framed in terms of two characters, A and B. But it seemed to me, as I listened to her describe the novel, that she was really much more interested in the relationship between A and a third character, C. I brought this up. She thought about my observations, and replied that she was of two minds: that there was still value in the current novel, but that I might be on to something important.

I wondered aloud about the possibility that her current novel might have to be abandoned in favor of a new one in which A and C got to interact properly. This is always a little presumptuous to say and very painful to hear, but it is the kind of reality-testing that creativity consultants need to engage in. Every writer has had the experience of holding on to a project for too long, even though he or she has been suspicious about the goodness or rightness of the work for some time. It therefore doesn't pay for a consultant to make believe that every project will work. But it is still always upsetting, discouraging, and even traumatic for the client to be confronted by such a possibility in a consultation session.

In a while the session ended. I wouldn't have hazarded a guess as to how helpful I had been, whether I had been right or wrong, or how ready this writer might be to entertain the possibilities we discussed. But when we met a month later she reported that the session had been very painful but also very useful. Between the first session and the second she had jettisoned the old novel and begun the new novel, a great deal of which she'd already completed. She was writing every day with enthusiasm and felt on track. On that positive note, we concluded our work together.

The moral? Pain is a central part of a writer's education. Pain is inevitable, as you discover that this piece must be rebuilt from the foundation up, that that piece is dead in the middle, that this third piece is a beautiful idea rottenly executed. Since pain is inevitable, fear it a little less. If you fear it too much, you won't be able to look at your work and you'll block. If you try to avoid the pain by doing something more pleasant, like eating chocolate or watching TV, you'll squander time and dig yourself into a hole. Instead, educate yourself about pain and about pain management.

EDUCATING YOURSELF
ABOUT THE BUSINESS OF WRITING

You educate yourself about writing by writing. But what about selling your writing? How do you educate yourself about that? Consider the following. John is a writer with a novel half-written. His friend Joyce works in sales. They have the following conversation, which John begins.

"I've decided to try to sell my book!"

"Great! What's your plan?"

"Well . . . I don't know."

"Do you have to prospect?"

"What does that mean?"

"Well, in my business I cold-call people I think might be interested in what I sell. I try to interest them over the phone—"

"God! I could never do that! Besides, the people who buy books would never take my call—"

"Who does buy books?"

"Well . . . I'm not sure. Editors, I suppose. Or publishers? I'm not sure what the difference is. Then there are literary agents . . . that's the ticket! They represent you and sell your book for you."

"Great! So, there's a list of them somewhere and you call them up? Or contact them on-line? Or is it better to write?"

"There are whole books full of their names. I suppose I could just start at 'A' . . . or 'Z,' for that matter!"

"Been there, done that! That can't be the best way. In sales, if you do things that cold you waste a lot of time and energy. You can maybe blanket a lot of people with a form letter and an advertising piece, but the results usually aren't that great. For a product like yours—"

"Don't call it a product!"

"Hush up. It is. For a product like yours, where you only have to sell one and not a thousand, you're not looking for lots of prospects, just the right few. You want somebody who's just right. What do you need in an agent?"

"That she wants me!"

"Yes, of course, and what else?"

"That she can sell!"

"Which means?"

"I don't know. That she sleeps with editors, who then owe her favors."

"Stop it. Be serious. If I understand this correctly, an agent is herself a salesperson. You're selling to her and then she's selling to somebody else. So, what I look for in a salesperson are people skills, marketing savvy, and a track record. I would think that you'd want an agent who's sold plenty of books, who knows the ropes, and who can communicate clearly."

"Sounds about right. Now . . . why would she want me?"

"Excellent question! You tell me. What are you selling her that she would want to resell?"

"Half a novel that sort of sucks."

"John—"

"That also has some undeniable strengths and a great deal of promise."

"John—"

"Well? I'm not kidding. That's the truth! My novel has its good points and its bad points."

"If I were an agent, I wouldn't feel too inspired or excited."

"There you go."

"Now don't mope. Tell me, if your novel were everything it ought to be, could you sell an agent on it then?"

"I have no idea."

"But the first step is getting your novel in great shape?"

"I don't know. I see books at Barnes & Noble that are pure garbage. So garbage must sell."

"John. Don't be cynical."

"I am saying a truthful thing. Goodness guarantees nothing and badness surely makes it into the marketplace."

"Is that going to be your mantra: 'Make it stink, win big!'?"

"I just read the other day, this writer was saying that if Tolstoy, Dostoevsky, James Joyce, or Virginia Woolf were writing today, not a one of them would get published. The marketplace has no space for them!"

"I wonder if that's true. But for argument's sake, let's say that it is. So, why would you make typewriters in an age of computers? Or quill pens? Why would you write Dostoevky-like if you *knew* no one would buy it?"

"I don't know. Why would you search for God when there's so much money to be made in the stock market?"

"Now, now."

"We may not have a common language."

"No, I think we do. It's like selling anything; some things are not that much wanted and some things are wanted a lot. A few people want to read poetry; millions want to read about angels and cats. So, you choose to write about angels and cats, or you figure out how to sell to your small market. If it's too small, well, that's the law of the marketplace—"

"—Of the jungle—"

"Of course. But let's say it's only small, as opposed to nonexistent. Let's say that you could sell a novel like yours—presuming you'd written it well—to, say, two thousand people. How could you pull that off? Would an agent want it?"

"Probably not."

"One of those big New York publishers?"

"Probably not."

"Could you publish it yourself?"

"Ugh!"

"Help me here, John."

"I hate all these implications!"

"Look at it this way. If you have any chance, then you need to maximize those chances. That must mean, write something good, rather than bad. . . . Don't you think?"

"Maybe."

"Then find the way to be the exception. Nine out of ten small businesses fail; the one that succeeds is the exception. Ninety-nine out a hundred firefighter applicants are rejected; the one who's hired is the exception. That's true everywhere, in every walk of life. When the odds are long, a person's job is to be the exception. So, let's work on that premise. You, John, are to be the exception."

"Thank you."

"I mean it!"

"All right. Thank you. I mean it, too."

"Then let's start over. . . ."

WRITERS' CONFERENCE PHOBIA

Writers' conferences can be educational experiences. Professionals in all fields attend conferences and conventions where they can meet the people they hope to learn from, network with, and sell to. But most writers, even though they would like to sell to agents and editors, do not attend writers' conferences where those agents and editors appear. Why don't they?

Writers argue that there are other ways of connecting with these people—through query letters, for the most part—and that the cost of attending can't really be justified. But the proof that money isn't the real issue is the fact that if you gave them a free pass, most still wouldn't attend. It turns out that many writers, if not the vast majority, are actually phobic about attending writers' conferences. They feel such conferences are to be avoided at all costs. They feel that way because:

* Most writers are basically shy.
* Their pride gets in the way (agents and editors should be coming to them!).
* They feel uncomfortable identifying themselves as writers. (At one conference, the keynote speaker asked the two hundred people in the audience to raise a hand if they felt like a "real writer." Only two people raised their hands, Jean Auel and me.)
* They may have to show their work and they may learn that it isn't good enough or wanted.
* They may have to talk to industry professionals, which prospect fills them with anxiety.
* They feel unprepared, too much like novices, unentitled to spend money on themselves on such "luxuries," skeptical about the value of the experience, skeptical about the motives and expertise of the presenters, angry and disappointed about what they will hear about the marketplace even before they hear it.
* They may have to talk about their work. As I mentioned before, I lead role playing workshops at writers' conferences where writers come up and role play writer-agent and writer-editor interactions. I see firsthand just how difficult it is for writers to tell an editor or an agent what their work's about in one or two clear sentences.

For these and other reasons, many writers are phobic about attending writers' conferences. They can't think about them clearly or decide in a rational way whether attending them is or isn't in their best interests. If you're anxious but understand the importance of networking and personal contacts in the writing world, try your hand at the following exercise.

Goal

To gain clarity about what writers' conferences are and whether they might be of value to you; to reduce your anxiety about attending them; to locate useful writers' conferences that serve your needs; to attend at least one; and to make the kinds of personal contacts with writers, agents, and editors that will serve your writing career.

Plan

Step 1. Start by thinking about writers' conferences with an open mind. Try to let go of old feelings of embarrassment, annoyance, anger, and so on. Try to let go of any fears you have about putting yourself or your work on display, about chit-chatting with agents and editors, about calling yourself a writer and mingling with other writers. Try to feel neither too prideful nor too small.

Step 2. Try to figure out what prevents you from attending writers' conferences. Is it that you don't consider yourself a "real" writer? Is it more that you feel that no one has anything to teach you or tell you? Are you unprepared to talk about your work or show your work? Is it more that the thought of interacting with editors and agents fills you with dread? Spend some time with yourself and see if you can unravel this mystery.

Step 3. Once you've figured out what sort of issue is really involved—pride, anxiety, self-image, etc.—ask yourself, "What is in my best interests to do? Even if the prospect of talking to editors fills me with dread, would it still be wise to stretch myself and attend a conference?" Your answer may still be no, but, having spoken your fears out loud, it may now be yes.

Step 4. Learn more about writers' conferences. Send away to several writers' conferences for their brochures. How about nature writing in Squaw Valley? Magazine writing in Aspen? Children's picture book writing in Arkansas? Travel writing in Alaska? Locate some intriguing conferences and learn all you can about them, including their track records of attracting solid faculties of published writers, agents, and editors. Remember that how you rate the faculty will depend in large measure on whether you are going to a conference more to improve your writing skills or to network with industry professionals. If your goal is primarily the former, you want successful writers and good teachers. If your goal is primarily the latter, you want proven agents and editors.

Step 5. If you decide to attend a conference, make all the necessary practical and emotional preparations. Plan how you will speak about your work. Rehearse your answers to the basic questions about yourself you will surely be asked.

Step 6. Actually attend a conference. Go with an open mind and an open heart. Try to do as little hiding as possible. Sign up for one-on-one meetings with agents and editors. Even if you have nothing to sell at the moment, make use of this opportunity to speak to these writing professionals about your ideas. See what interests them and what fails to interest them. See how they react to you and your presentation style. Take chances and make connections.

Step 7. When you return home, take some time to process what transpired. You may be left with many strong feelings, both positive and negative. You may have been unimpressed by this agent or that editor, or insulted by some remark made to you about your writing or your presentation skills. But you may also have been invited by this agent or that editor to submit materials, or praised for your writing sample. Do your best to clear the air of any negative feelings that linger on as you work to retain whatever useful information you may have learned.

Step 8. Follow up. If a particular editor seemed sharp, approachable, or warm to you, and her house publishes the kind of work you're in the middle of writing, request her house's catalog and submission guidelines. Write her a personal letter, thanking her for her time and advising her that you mean to approach her with your work.

Also follow up on your own thoughts and feelings. Do you have a different sense of how the marketplace operates now? What new steps will you need to take, given your increased understanding? Do you have the sense that you need to improve your presentation skills? How will you do that? Take the time to learn from this important experience.

MAKING CHOICES

Your editor wonders if you envision the book that you're proposing more as a hardcover book or more as a trade paperback. You reply that:

    (a) You're happy to leave that decision up to her.

    (b) You wonder if she might not want to discuss this with your agent.

    (c) You see the book more as a trade paperback, because its lower price will make it accessible to a greater number of people.

    (d) You see the book more as a hardcover, because you think that it could gain an initial following and some word-of-mouth interest that way, which would help the subsequent paperback version. And the higher royalty rates of a hardback feel like a significant bonus.

    (e) You aren't sure how to think about the distinction and wonder if she can talk you through it.

When writers are invited to participate in the publishing process—which happens relatively rarely but more often when the writer is a sensible, knowledgable collaborator—they almost always feel they don't know how to think about the issues being raised. You're asked if you think the book should have an index—well, what exactly are the pros and cons of the matter? You're asked if you'd prefer to have the editor find ten thousand words to remove from your too-long manuscript, or whether you'd like to do that yourself—well, what are the pros and cons of the alternatives in this case?

The phone rings, your mind is on your cat's diarrhea and your new novel, and your editor says, "We're having a meeting in a few minutes and I just wanted to get your input. We're thinking of changing the title of your book from *Gone with the Wind* to *Smoke over Atlanta*, taking out Chapter 3 so we can price the book at $16.95, and going with an arty, hip cover done in shades of peach and rose. What do you think?" Well, what *do* you think?

Part of a writer's education is experiencing any number of these sudden crises and learning from such experiences how to anticipate the kinds of questions that arise—always suddenly, it seems—in the sales and publication processes. This means educating oneself about contracts, especially with regard to the points that matter—about discounted royalty rates, subsidiary rights, delivery dates, and the like—and about the kinds of surprises that arise in the publication process, from the not-uncommon perceived need to shorten a book, in order to price it more competitively, to last-minute worries about the book's title.

You do want to be able to answer such questions and meet such surprises, stating clearly your preferences and the rationale for your preferences, rather than throwing up your hands and leaving the matter to the mercy and wisdom of your editor or other marketplace players. It is unreasonable to suppose that you will do this well at the beginning of your career. Your goal is to get better and better at anticipating and responding to the flash fires that break out when your manuscript meets up with reality.

ROLE PLAY:
Everyday Cross-Examinations

Person A: You are a writer currently working on a book. (Please try to think of some book you actually have worked on, are working on, or have even completed. If you've never worked on a book, try to come up with a book idea right now and imagine that you've launched into it.) You are attending an agents' panel at a book fair and you have made a pact with yourself to talk about your work with at least one of the agents present. The panel discussion is over and the time is now. You go up to the agent you've singled out, introduce yourself, and let him/her know about your current project.

Person B: You are a literary agent. You have just been part of an agents' panel at a book fair, and now you are mingling with members of the audience. Naturally, these writers want to pitch their projects to you, and you, for your part, are looking for good projects to represent while at the same time needing to fend off projects that don't interest you. This writer has cornered you to talk about his/her project. The questions you need answered are:

1 What's the book about? (You want a really clear sentence or two. If you don't get what you want, ask the writer to be clearer, more succinct.)

2. Who's the audience for the book? (How is the book slanted, what well-known books has this audience read recently, what does the book offer readers that they will want?)

3. What are this writer's credentials? (What has this writer written before, what has he/she written in this area or genre, what's been published, how well have his/her published works sold?)
4. Who does this writer see publishing this book? (Does the writer have specific publishing houses or editors in mind? If not, why not?)
5. How much of the book is written? (You need the answer in number of words, not number of pages, since page counts can be misleading.)
6. When will the book be finished? (You need the answer in number of months or years, not just "soon" or "in a long time.")
7. Is there a book proposal (for nonfiction) or a synopsis (for fiction) ready to show? If not, when will it be ready?
8. What will the writer do to help market, advertise, and support the book? (If the writer has no ideas or only vague ideas here, demand more concreteness.)

Please make sure that you get answers to all of these questions. If you are not satisfied with the answers you get, please ask the writer to clarify what he/she means. Be a little on the helpful and generous side, but remain essentially skeptical and demanding. If you like what you hear, ask to see the project. If you don't, say you don't.

Debriefing Questions

Questions for the writer to answer:

1. What was the experience like for you?
2. Did any of the questions feel illogical or unexpected?
3. Would rehearsing answers to questions like these have helped you make a better presentation?
4. What was your experience of anxiety like? Was it high? Even surprisingly high? What might you do to help yourself meet such moments with less anxiety (e.g., rehearse or practice with a friend, manufacture as many opportunities to chat with agents as possible, learn a breathing technique to help calm yourself down)?
5. What did you learn about the difficulties inherent in speaking about your work?

Questions for the agent to answer:

1. What was the experience like for you?
2. Do you now have a better sense of what agents want and need and how they operate?
3. What impressed you about this writer's presentation?

4. Where was improvement particularly needed?

5. What did you learn about presenting your own work?

Questions for the observers to answer:

1. What especially struck you about the interaction?

2. Where was the writer strong in his/her presentation? Where was he/she weak?

3. Did the agent seem reasonable? Unreasonable? Both?

4. What looks to be the most important thing for a writer to remember about such interactions?

5. What did you learn from this role play about presenting your own work?

(We will revisit this role play in Chapter 9.)

FOOD FOR THOUGHT

"I regret German very much, history I can read alone, French is still going on, the rules of geography and grammar are tiresome, and there is no general word to express the feelings I have always entertained towards arithmetic."—Beatrix Potter

If a formal education counts for little, what counts for a lot?

"When I stepped from hard manual work to writing, I just stepped from one kind of hard work to another."—Sean O'Casey

Do you need writing to be easy? Are you able to change your mind about that?

"The best ideas come unexpectedly from a conversation or a common activity like watering the garden. These can get lost or slip away if not acted on when they occur."—Ruth Asawa

When a writing idea unexpectedly comes to you, do you write it down immediately? If not, why not?

"The suspense of a novel is not only in the reader, but in the novelist, who is intensely curious about what will happen to the hero."—Mary McCarthy

Are you curious enough about the life of your work?

"When I want to read a good book, I write one."—Benjamin Disraeli

Are your own books your best education?

"It is only when we forget all learning that we begin to know."—Henry David Thoreau

What do you need to unlearn?

*"When I read my first book, I started writing my
first book. I have never not been writing."*—Gore Vidal
Is this your story, too? What does it signify?

*"The perfect place for a writer is in the hideous roar of a city, with men
making a new road under his window in competition with a barrel organ,
and on the mat a man waiting for the rent."*—Henry Vollam Morton
Have you learned to write despite distractions?

*"Most authors are looking for tragedy without finding it. They remember
personal little stories which aren't tragedy."*—Louis-Ferdinand Celine
Does only tragedy educate? What else educates?

*"At a certain point, you have to go to the edge of the cliff and jump—
put your ideas into a form, share that form with others."*—Meredith Monk
Are you prepared to jump? When will you be?

*"You ask for the distinction between the terms 'Editor' and 'Publisher': an editor
selects manuscripts; a publisher selects editors."*—M. Lincoln Schuster
**Do you understand who's who in the publishing industry? Is that an important
education to acquire?**

*"A small press is an attitude, a kind of anti-commerciality. The dollars come
second, the talent and the quality of the writing come first. If the presses wanted
to make money, they'd be out there selling cookbooks."*—Bill Henderson
**Do you understand what a publisher's size means? Is that important knowledge
to acquire?**

*"Read, read, read. Read everything—trash, classics, good
and bad, and see how they do it. Read!"*—William Faulkner
Do you still read? What are you learning these days?

"In the dark time, the eye begins to see."—Theodore Roethke
What have pain and suffering taught you?

"Eventually quantity will make for quality."—Ray Bradbury
Are you writing enough?

3
A Writer's Craft

What do we mean by "the craft" of writing?

To pursue the analogy of the first chapter, where I likened writing to speaking, I think that the difference between ordinary writing and well-crafted writing is the difference between speaking and oratory. It isn't coincidental that the same skills are employed by both the good speaker and the good writer. For thousands of years we have called these skills "rhetorical."

Rhetoric isn't just the province of the Latin teacher and the debater but the province of every writer who wants to craft her measure of truth, beauty, and goodness. The dictionary defines rhetoric as "the art of effective expression and the persuasive use of language" and a rhetorician as "an eloquent speaker or writer." We could do much worse than define the craft of writing as the writer's ability to use language effectively, persuasively, and eloquently.

At the heart of eloquent writing and eloquent speaking is strong thinking. Every piece of eloquent writing is a compelling argument, made up of the kinds of rhetorical devices debaters learn: cause-and-effect arguments, comparisons and contrasts, supporting evidence, and so on. Eloquent writing, whether it is prose or poetry, fiction or nonfiction, is logical: characters do not act out of character, words do not change their meaning unless the writer intends them to change. It is also human: its arguments are built on human foundations, on human experience, out of the whole cloth of the human predicament. The writer analyzes, synthesizes, and evaluates, just as if she were doing science or engineering, but her subject is her species.

How does a writer become eloquent? By wanting to. She writes; she erases; she does better. She is not satisfied until the illogic is corrected, until the analogy works, until the argument persuades. She writes weak things but doesn't stoop to defend them; instead she grows angry and demands of herself that she do better. She writes and writes and writes. She signs a pact in her own blood that she will write well; then she keeps her promise.

WRITING ANYTHING

It was 1975. I was returning from a year in Europe and passing through New York when I stopped at the house of a friend of mine in Brooklyn Heights. It turned out that she was writing a book to order for her brother-in-law, an entrepreneur who at that split second was dabbling as a middle-man in the ghostwriting/tax write-off trade.

My friend was writing an "inflation fighting handbook." Previously she had written a cookbook (instant meals in your blender, for the college student) and an unauthorized biography of a celebrity. She was behind schedule and wondered if I wanted to write a chapter of the inflation fighting handbook. I told her that I knew about not having money but not about fighting inflation. She said that the two were identical and that I could have an easy chapter, on getting free things from the government. Every inflation fighting handbook had a chapter on getting free things from the government.

I wrote the chapter (I don't remember how, but I'm sure it wasn't pretty) and passed the test: getting words down on paper fast. Her brother-in-law was impressed. He offered me my own book to write, a mystery. The phone conversation arranging the deal went like this:

> "Write one called *The Black Narc*," he said.
>
> "*The Black Narc*?" I said.
>
> "Right."
>
> "You mean, about a narcotics detective who is black?"
>
> "Could be. That's up to you."
>
> "You mean . . . ?"

What he meant, it turned out, was that I could write anything at all, just so long as I called it *The Black Narc*. The title was everything. Where had the title come from? Intense market research? Feverish brainstorming?

> "Why *The Black Narc*?" I asked.
>
> "Something like that was in last week's *T.V. Guide*. I think. It doesn't matter."
>
> "I see."

> "I have no fancy ideas about poetry. It doesn't come to you on the wings of a dove. It's something you work hard at."
>
> —Louise Bogan

Do you admit that you have to work at your craft?

The details of the deal were remarkably simple. No eight-page book contracts, no addenda about audio rights, not even a mention of the name of the publisher.

"Can you write it in two months?" he said. "For $2000? Then I'll get you another one to write and another one for as long as you like."

Yes, I said. I got to San Francisco, where I meant to live, and wrote *The Black Narc*. I loved that book. I made the black narc Jewish and to fulfill the promise of the title had him avenge the death of his buddy, an honest-to-god black narc. There were acid blindings, shotguns, neo-Nazis, drug-filled warehouses. I really loved that book.

Then I did a second book on the same terms ("Write one called *The Kingston Papers* for another $2000"), which I decided would be about the American Medical Association suppressing a miraculous, mysterious cure for cancer. Then I did one on singles' bars in twenty-nine major American cities, God knows how. I got two writer friends mysteries to write—we were becoming a little book factory. Then I did a book on biorhythms, which appeared under the name of a well-known clinical psychologist.

This last one hurt and soured me on ghostwriting. It was worth $5000 to write, a princely sum. After researching the subject I came up with my thesis: that biorhythms, those supposedly exact cycles of emotional and intellectual variability invented by Freud's nose doctor and cocaine connection Wilhelm Fleiss, were bogus and a joke, but that if you wanted to have fun with them, here was the kind of fun you could have.

In my naivete—I was only twenty-eight or twenty-nine, just out of adolescence—I thought that since no one had told me what I was supposed to do with the subject ("Now write a book on biorhythms—it's $5000 for this one") I could debunk it if I liked. Wrong! The book appeared (from a large, well-known publisher) with some strategic editing and a new thesis: that biorhythms were a proven, scientifically accurate system of prediction. Use the system to pick the best day to do your calculus homework or leave your lover.

As I say, that hurt. So I stopped ghostwriting.

As I was stopping, I turned down a cure-your-arthritis book, which, however, a friend of mine happily undertook to write. Soon it appeared with a celebrity's name on it. The celebrity took to the talk-show circuit explaining his arthritis cures, cures that my friend had dreamed up in Paris while listening to the Rolling Stones. I also turned down a twelve-book Harlequin-like romance deal (one romance a month, $1000 per romance) and other projects I only vaguely remember. How to buy an Oriental rug? Inflation fighters' handbook #99? Few were actually meant to sell. Many were tax write-offs for somebody or other. But others came out from big publishers, actually appearing as the front-list titles of major houses.

Are black narcs still being merrily transformed into Jewish narcs in the hands of young writers thrilled to be paid for writing? I don't know. I have no idea who is hiding behind whom on the shelves of Borders and Barnes & Noble, or exactly what sins I committed in my brief life as a ghostwriter. But I do know that I recall Jimmy Jacobs the Jewish narc with great fondness. I still think it miraculous that, whatever predicament he found himself in, he always had just the right gadget in his pocket to effect his escape.

The lesson? There are several. But the one I want to underline is the following: get good at the craft of writing by writing (just about) **anything**.

A One-Day Writing Workshop

The following is a workshop I've been giving periodically for the past fifteen years. It's a simple workshop: essentially I do nothing but invite writers to write. Yet it has remarkable effects. Writers who've been blocked for months and even years begin to write again. Writers who've only vaguely contemplated writing a book manage to frame the book and launch into it in the course of a single day.

The secret for the success of the workshop is the following. I "hold the silence" and "hold the intention" in the room in a way that quiets the noisy, self-critical, fearful part of a writer's personality. I act as a calming, reassuring, seductive presence, seducing writers to forget about their worries and to begin writing.

Try out this workshop whenever you like. Use it when you're about to begin a book, when you're stuck on a chapter, or when you want to choose between one writing project versus another. Use it to get the last poem or two in a series done or when your article deadline approaches. Use it by yourself or gather together a small group. Facilitation amounts to nothing more than quietly following the instructions. Remember: to craft something is nothing more than to work with integrity and ever-growing skill.

> *"A bad book is as much labor to write as a good one; it comes as sincerely from the author's soul."*
>
> —Aldous Huxley
>
> **Do you understand that the goodness of the work can't be guaranteed beforehand?**

First the agenda for the workshop:

Beginnings (9:00–9:15 a.m.)
Mission Piece (9:15–10:30 a.m.)
Break (10:30–10:45 a.m.)
Reading Your Mission Piece (10:45–11:00 a.m.)
Continuing (11:00 a.m.–12:00 noon)
Lunch (12:00 noon–1:00 p.m.)
Returning to Your Mission Piece (1:00–2:00 p.m.)
Reading Your Mission Piece (2:00–2:30 p.m.)
Break (2:30–2:45 p.m.)
Continuing and Completing (2:45–4:00 p.m.)
Looking Forward (4:00–4:30 p.m.)

Beginnings *(9:00–9:15 a.m.)*

Today is a day to work and to feel yourself in action. You will spend today with your writing. Even on breaks, even as you eat your lunch, try to remain with your writing.

Let's begin by creating a writing bubble.

Seat yourself comfortably. Shut your eyes. Attune to your breathing. Let go of all that has no place here, all that you don't need at this moment. Begin to feel the presence of your own writing. You and your words are together. Build a bubble around you and them. Create a rich, protective environment. You can let in what you want, you can keep out what you want, but inside this bubble you and your words are together.

Feel being inside. Here you can write. The world will keep its distance. The bubble is transparent but real. It allows in light, it allows in whatever you need. Inside it you and your words can be together. When you're ready, open your eyes. But hold the feeling and the fact that you are now in your own writing world, connected to your own resources.

It is time to work. It is time to write. It is time to complete a significant piece of writing, your mission piece for the day.

Mission Piece *(9:15–10:30 a.m.)*

Today you are working on a particular piece. It is a piece you're about to begin or one that you've been working on for some time. It may be something in between: a piece that you've thought about for a long time, made notes for, but never begun. The first step is to really decide that this is the piece you mean to tackle today. You want to approach it with enthusiasm and feel as if you're on a mission.

Imagine a bookshelf full of works you've written. Visualize a row of novels, nonfiction books, poetry volumes, bound screenplays, bound articles, bound essays, or some combination of these. Feel the weight, the goodness, the personality of each of these books. Feel the way you managed to bring ideas to fruition in each book. Some of the books are thicker, some thinner. Some you found easier to write, some harder. Some were well-received, some were ignored. But each is a real work into which you poured love and sweat. Each is valuable, commendable, praiseworthy.

Be with that shelf of books. Attune to the importance of each book, to the importance of the whole; feel the joy at what you accomplished; see the titles on the spines. These are the past, present, and future fruits of your writing labors. Feel the breadth of your body of work. Only one book could be written at a time, and when you were writing one you couldn't be writing another. This shelf represents the choices you had to make at different moments. But ultimately you didn't have to choose one book over another. Ultimately you could write them all.

Still, you had to write the books one at a time. Start toward the present moment. What, from the shelf, do you want to work on today? Stand up. Walk in a wide circle, holding in consciousness the piece you want to write now and all the other pieces that may have flooded into consciousness as a result of this exercise. These may be different chapters of the same book, different aspects of the same subject, unrelated articles, pieces reflecting your different but equally real passions. In a minute you will have to choose and commit to a mission piece. But not yet. Walk for a minute, letting yourself understand all the rich possibilities available to you and letting today's piece choose itself.

Sit back down. Generate from your thoughts a list of titles that reflect what you learned from seeing your collected works and from holding them in consciousness. Once you've generated the list, take a thirty-second time-out, but remain focused and present. Now, look at your list. Each title has a life to it. Feel the life of each one. One may feel especially rich but also especially difficult. A second may feel easy to write but not weighty enough for today. A third may feel like the richest of all, but just beyond your capabilities to write. Write a brief, impressionistic description of each title, just a sentence or two or even just a few words.

No doubt you'd supposed before starting this exercise that you'd already decided on the piece you'd be writing today. But after this exercise you may have a different feeling. Now that you've had the chance to bring other works into consciousness, it is time to make a decision. It is time to choose your mission piece.

Breathe, decide, and commit.

The pieces you have chosen not to write today will not wither away and die. They will transform themselves out of sight and continue to exist. Hold on to them, but also let them go. They are not lost, but they are also not present. The only thing present is your mission piece, the piece you are now committed to writing. Be thankful that you now have a piece into which to pour your enthusiasm.

Begin now. Do not make lists. Do not make notes. Do not make an outline. Write in real connection to the material. Just write. Do not suppose that you will be unable to say what you want to say. Do not keep your distance. Just write. Write for the next hour.

Break *(10:30–10:45 a.m.)*

Stop now and take a break. Do not reread what you've written. Do not begin to think that it's bad. Do not begin to think anything negative. Just take a real break. At the same time, keep the writing in mind. Or just keep writing right through your break if the writing is pressing. Always write, if the writing is pressing. But do not reread even a word of what you've written so far, not even just to "find your place." Either take a real break or continue letting your mission piece out.

If you are on break now, congratulate yourself. You worked! If you're still writing, stay committed and focused. But do take at least a little break before your next stint. Break for at least a minute. When you do, congratulate yourself. You worked!

Reading Your Mission Piece *(10:45–11:15 a.m.)*

Now is the time to read what you've written. Remember that you are committed to this piece; ugly sentences or poorly expressed ideas will not derail you. Read with an appraising eye but not with a sinking heart. This is a draft; this is a beginning; you will make this piece work. Do not let yourself get discouraged.

Some of it will seem strong and some of it will seem weak. None of that matters right now. What matters is that you stay inside the writing. Did you write from the inside-out, as if you were deep in the belly of the beast, or from the outside-in, as if you were viewing the beast from a great distance?

Take a one-minute timeout, but remain focused and present. Try to answer the question, "Was I inside or outside when I wrote these pages?" If the answer is "outside," see if you can lower the wall between you and the material. Imagine crawling into the belly of the beast. Picture the darkness, the smells, the intimacy, the warmth. See if you can get inside. If the answer was "inside," congratulations.

Continuing *(11:15 a.m.–12:00 noon)*

You may be feeling tired, worn out, even a little ill. You're doing real work and that takes its toll. Accept any discomfort you feel and lose yourself in the work. Just continue.

Lunch *(12:00 noon–1:00 p.m.)*

Have a simple lunch. Relax from your writing but still keep your writing in mind. If a bit of writing comes to you, write it down, but try to feel yourself on break. Relax, smile, laugh, enjoy your food, take a walk. If you're part of a group, chat with your fellow writers about this and that. Come back early or, at worst, on time, to symbolize your readiness and willingness to resume.

Returning to Your Mission Piece *(1:00–2:00 p.m.)*

You've been away from your mission piece for an hour, but not very far away. It remains close at hand, available, alive, ready to be worked on. If you need to, reread parts that you wrote in the morning. If you need to, make notes, do a little outlining, do whatever you feel it necessary to do.

If you feel blocked, read the following list. As you read each item on the list, vigorously cross it out. Cross out all these lies. Then get back to work.

1. I don't really know enough to do this piece.
2. I have nothing to say.
3. Whoever reads this piece will see that it's bad.
4. I don't know why I ever thought I could write.
5. This isn't real writing.
6. This will never get published.
7. I'm wasting my time.
8. I'm incredibly untalented.
9. I'm incredibly unoriginal.
10. This is bringing up feelings I can't stand to feel.
11. This is bringing up thoughts I can't stand to think about.
12. I can't focus.
13. I don't have what it takes.
14. This piece stinks.
15. I have no idea what I'm doing.

Obliterate each of these lies and then write for an hour. Stay with it—don't take any breaks.

Reading Your Mission Piece *(2:00–2:30 p.m.)*

You may like your afternoon's writing. You may not. Try to put judgments out of your mind and concentrate on what you want to write next, during your last writing stint of the day. Do you want to do some revising? Do you want to plow forward? Do you want to leap to another scene or another chapter? Do you want to write something entirely different? Breathe, make a strong choice, commit to it, and get ready for some more productive writing.

Break *(2:30–2:45 p.m.)*

Take a complete break from the writing. Think about other things or about nothing at all. Smell the roses. Stretch. Make funny noises. Dance with the cat. Let the writing go. When the break is over, it will come back.

Continuing and Completing (2:45–4:00 p.m.)

This is your last writing stint of the day. Work intensely, but also savor that the end is near. You will have written for four and a half hours today. That's terrific! Just as importantly, you've looked your work in the eye, confronted it, faced up to it, and learned from it. Accept your fatigue and woolly-headedness and write deeply and powerfully for another hour and fifteen minutes.

Looking Forward (4:00–4:30 p.m.)

The work is not done until it is done. So, before you stop for the day, reread your last writing chunk and make any last notes. Jot down your ideas for revisions or elaborations, ideas for the next scene or the next chapter. Then let the writing go. Congratulate yourself on having worked and turn your attention to an evening of celebration.

CRAFT AND THE "MULTIPLE IDENTITIES" OF THE WRITER

Melissa Bay Mathis writes and illustrates children's books. She recently wrote and illustrated *Animal House*, and has illustrated *The Turtle and the Moon*, *The Velveteen Rabbit*, and *What a Wonderful Day to Be a Cow*, among many other titles. She provided the following piece.

On the Road to a Picture Book

A true picture book is much like a movie. Readers are dropped into a created world where an emotional journey using many senses has been orchestrated for them. Hopefully, they'll close the book with a sense of transformation.

Yet movies are made by large groups of people having different talents, strengths, and job descriptions, and picture books are often made basically by one mind. The picture book creator has to look inside to find the required multiple personalities to fill a whole roster of jobs.

Once hired on, this crazy bunch of characters takes off on a wild creative road trip together. Everyone has to take a turn at the wheel, but also to step aside when it's someone else's turn to drive. And the book's creator has to manage the bunch, keep them all happy and working, and break up the inevitable fights. Not an easy task, when you consider these unlikely travelmates. . . .

The Collector *likes to eavesdrop, ask questions, and squirrel away details for future use. She likes quirks, idiosyncratic qualities, contradictions, unique personalities. She rules over a huge database of possible material, but hates to choose one gem out of the group, for fear of leaving something out.*

The Beginner's job is to travel into the void where no book exists, *and find a place to land. The seed of a book must be a truly sound idea, since no amount of crafting of words or pictures will save a book if that crucial element is not strong. It takes so much energy to make this large commitment to something that moments before did not exist, that, having acted, she's ready to hibernate and hand the wheel over to the others.*

The Scriptwriter *slides into the driver's seat and starts generating words meant to guide the reader through the experience in time that is the book. Standing over her shoulder is the* Wordsmith, *wanting each word to be economical, elegant, right. They wrangle with each other sometimes. The Scriptwriter only wants language that drives the book forward, helps readers know where they are, and maintains the right pace. The Wordsmith craves delicious, unique words that evoke smells, sounds, tastes, feelings. She plays with words as sounds to hear again and again, since picture books are read this way.*

Across the aisle sits the Queen of Continuity. *No one picture, phrase, or event matters as much to the Queen as the overall flow of the book. Her favorite medium is the turn of the page. Her mind can take a set of still images and play them in her head as a movie, speeding up here, slowing down there, cutting things out. The* Camerawoman, *next to her, likes the helicopter view also. She loves interesting angles, and invents scenarios to maximize the emotional impact of the book. She sees the whole world through the frame of the edges of the page, and each spread is a puzzle to solve elegantly. Her sidekick, the* Painter, *stands by, whining to be allowed to take one of those spreads and play with it. The Painter doesn't talk a lot, wants to get her hands on things, can't explain why she chooses one color over another. Watching all of this is the* Draftswoman, *a 2B pencil in one hand and a kneaded eraser in the other. She knows that the Camerawoman and the Continuity Queen will have to work out their differences before she can happily obsess about her favorite topics: anatomy, values, and perspective. She's firm about one thing. The pesky Painter will just have to* wait *to play.*

The Draftswoman *has a best friend: the* Reference Maven, *who likes to take trips and wants to experience everything first hand. She does not trust memory and has to look freshly at anything that may end up in her book. In her mind, there is no such thing as too many reference books, and she buys them with abandon (don't try to talk budget to her). She's only encouraged in this by the* Perfectionist, *who can't tell time and can't read calendars but has an eagle eye for weak spots in the writing or art that could use improving.*

Should you hesitantly suggest that there may not be time for all this scrutiny, you risk incurring her tremendous wrath. Possibly she might hog the driver's seat for decades if she wasn't forcibly ejected by . . .

The Time Dominatrix, *who has such a fine sense of time that she can actually feel the tremors of a deadline that is fully six months away. The other team members put deadlines and alien ship landings in the same category; sure, their arrival would generate excitement, but it's nothing to worry about now. She herds them all on, occasionally calling for back-up from her buddy, the* Finisher.

The Finisher *is a close cousin to the Beginner, although they don't understand each other at all. The Beginner thrives in the clear cold air of No Book Yet while the Finisher has never known a world without this book in it. The Finisher is at peace with the work as it stands right now. She knows that the book will not truly live until it is in the hands of readers. She used to argue constantly with the Perfectionist, the Wordsmith, the Draftswoman, the Painter. They feel cut off by her, limited, that she doesn't understand how much more they could do if they only had more time. She has stopped trying to explain anything to them. She repeats her mantra (FedEx, FedEx, FedEx) and stands firm, tapping her foot, surrounded by packaging materials.*

Only one more passenger remains. Up till now, this one's been content to hang around the back of the bus, holding court, making jokes. But once the Finisher finishes, it's the Publicizer's *turn. She loves to talk, whether to a large audience or a long line of strangers at a book signing, and needs no time alone or to be quiet. While the others wear old clothes and don't remember to get a haircut, she's been seen in clothes that match. She talks about "her" book, but it's obvious that anyone this social could never have stayed alone long enough to create a book. Does she reveal the bitter struggles among the group, the disagreements, the times the bus almost ran off the road? Is she telling the whole story? Probably not. Yet the others put up with her, because, to tell the truth, they don't want to have to get up on that stage. Let her do it!*

Finally the bus arrives at its destination: a new book is out in the world. Time for a party! Of course, this motley crew has varying ideas of how to celebrate. The Publicizer's popping champagne, a lamp shade on her head. The Perfectionist prefers espresso and has to be stopped from finding flaws with the finished product. The Reference Maven is spreading out maps, convincing the Collector to come along on a trip. The Painter traces patterns in the dip and arranges the crudités in interesting configurations. And even before the party's over, the Beginner gets that far-away look in her eyes and wanders off, ready to reach into the void and begin again. . . .

MAKING CHOICES

Your current poem is complete, except for one word. Do you:

    (a) Wait for the word to come, even if it takes sixteen years?

    (b) Write out a list of synonyms, make a choice, and call the poem complete for now?

    (c) Bring up the thesaurus function of your computer spell check program and choose a word at random?

    (d) Rewrite the poem so that the need for that word vanishes?

    (e) Circulate the poem with the word missing and ask readers to fill in the blank?

> *"Even in the works of the greatest master we find moments when the organic sequence fails and a skillful join must be made, so that the parts appear as a completely welded whole."*
>
> —Peter Ilich Tchaikovsky
>
> **Are you skilled at making the necessary joins in your writing? Do you recognize the need for such craftsmanship?**

Writing is part mystery and part joinery. We're used to calling this distinction "art" and "craft," but what we really mean is that the resolution of the problem that writers set themselves when they begin a new piece requires a variety of attitudes with respect to knowing.

The writer has the sense that she knows where she's going when she starts out—that is, she has some intuitive sense of a destination and maybe even an intuitive sense of what the journey will look like. But she doesn't have anything like a blueprint. She has an intuition and a mandate but she must accept that she is working in the dark; she must suspend her desire to force herself to move in a pre-set direction and must hold tight to a belief in the process. She opens herself to the mysterious not-knowing of the creative process and hopes that the words she puts down are the right words, that they are matching her intuitive intentions and will read right when she rereads them.

But that rereading begins virtually instantly, as soon as even a few words have come together. Right away, the writer has to appraise the work as it grows and demand that it go in the appropriate direction. This is a fine paradox: she has to allow for process, letting the work grow and be, while also and at the same time demanding that it do what it is meant to do. She has to know even as she doesn't know and even as she doesn't want to know. She has to apply the tools of conscious knowing to the work, not turning a blind eye its way and not just hoping that it's progressing nicely. She has to actually read it and examine it for cracks and discolorations and respond to her own worries about the direction it's taking, even as she whispers to herself, "Stay alive, work, stay free, stay mysterious."

This can be done. But so many challenges arise along the way! You handle one and you handle the next and you handle the next and there you are, still left one word short. The lack of that last word epitomizes the process. You have been building and building and now for the want of a nail the house will not stand. Can something substitute for that nail? Must you wait for that nail to be delivered? What if the delivery never comes? Can you make a nail out of a sow's ear? Must you deconstruct the house and start all over again?

Go back to the world of mystery and silence. With luck, the word you want will come, maybe in an hour, maybe while you're doing the dishes, maybe early next week. If it will not come, there you are. You are missing a nail and have a painful choice to make. Waiting sixteen years is one choice; using the second-best word is another. Choose, and then live with your choice.

Sisyphus Smiles

The craft of writing is real work, and sometimes even grueling and maddening work. So why bother?

Writers bother because writing is a freedom attained. The writer lucky enough to recognize that writing is a freedom attained smiles a secret smile, a smile that reflects her felt freedom and sense of accomplishment, even as she works endlessly hard. Just as Sisyphus could not free himself from his endless labors but could still revel in the small freedoms he retained, so the writer cannot free herself from the creative process, with all its demands, anxieties, and pitfalls, but can still smile at the extraordinary human freedom that the very act of writing secures. Writing secures freedom, even though the process of writing can be as demanding as a stint at hard labor.

Think of the piece you're currently working on. Instead of holding it as a burden or an ugly mess, smile. Smile at your luck. You are exercising your voice, exercising your freedom. Practice that smile; really smile it. Of course, sometimes life will deal you heavy blows and your smile of freedom will vanish. Sometimes the work will shackle you and you'll groan. But if you invite the smile back and fully expect it to return, then it will, signaling that you are again ready to write, that you are again free, that you again matter.

ROLE PLAY:
An Editor with News

Person A:. You are a nonfiction writer who six weeks ago turned in a draft of your nonfiction book to your editor. The book was sold on the basis of a proposal and this is the first chance your editor has had to see how your ideas have come together. You are hoping that the manuscript is acceptable, with perhaps only a little cosmetic rewriting necessary. To be sure, you have some reservations about the book, but you're not sure that your editor will. You've been anxiously waiting to hear from him/her to get his/her reaction; finally you decide to call to see if he/she has gotten around to reading it yet.

> "I have written—
> often several
> times—every word I
> have ever published.
> My pencils outlast
> their erasers."
>
> —Vladimir Nabokov
>
> **Do you have a healthy
> relationship with
> the revision process?**

Person B:. You are an editor who is usually very circumspect in your dealings with writers. You tend to reject even poorly conceived, poorly written proposals with an "It's just not for us"; you rarely criticize a writer's work when you're on the phone with him/her, saving your observations either for a carefully crafted letter or for margin notes on the writer's manuscript. But with this writer, whose nonfiction proposal you bought a year ago, who turned in the manuscript six weeks ago, who's called for an update, and who's clearly hoping for a thumbs-up, you decide to speak what's on your mind. The manuscript is much less good than you had hoped, whole chapters make no sense, the book has no arc, the writing is wooden in places and glib in others, and you even have the suspicion that these flaws can't be corrected. In fact, the book may turn out to be unpublishable. Let the writer know what's on your mind, being as kind or as cruel as you like.

Debriefing Questions

Questions for the writer to answer:

1. What was the experience like for you?
2. Could you hear the specific things your editor was saying, or could you only hear that you were being criticized?
3. Did you experience this as a small setback or an irremediable failure? Did it help your feelings any to remember that technically this was only a "first draft"?

4. Did you feel that your editor helped you understand how to go about fixing what he/she believed needed fixing? Was he/she better at telling you what was wrong than at explaining what could be done to improve the book?
5. Did you experience this as a personal failure or as a failure of craft? Do you feel that by working at the craft of revising you could bring this book up to speed? Or do you feel as if the book's doomed?

Questions for the editor to answer:

1. What was the experience like for you?
2. Did you have the sense that the writer could hear what you were saying? What suggested that he/she could? What suggested that he/she couldn't?
3. Do you think that this conversation ruptured and ruined your relationship with this writer? Whether it did or didn't, is it your belief that writers should learn to take such news stoically? Or are they entitled to feel upset?
4. Did you have the sense that you were trying to express the idea that this book had a correctable craft problem or did you feel as if you were telling this writer that he/she had screwed up and that all was lost?
5. Is this a conversation to have on the phone? What are the pluses and minuses of handling this matter on the phone?

Questions for the observers to answer:

1. What especially struck you about the interaction?
2. Could you gauge the writer's reaction to the editor's news? Did the writer react defensively, aggressively, with instant sadness or depression, with anger?
3. Although the conversation was putatively about how well or poorly the book was crafted, did it feel like a conversation about craft?
4. Say the writer had told the editor, "Well, there appear to be many things to correct and, with your help, I will correct them." Might that have angled the conversation toward a discussion of craft? Is it likely that any writer, hoping to get a clean bill of health about a project, could switch gears and instantly reconcile himself/herself to a massive revision process?
5. If you found yourself in similar circumstances, waiting to hear from an editor about a book of yours, would you be more or less likely to call after witnessing this interaction? If you planned to call, how might you prepare yourself?

Q & A

How can I improve my writing?

Improve your thinking.

Books end up weak and unconvincing because the writer has had trouble with his ideas and arguments. This is not to say that the writer was stupid. The writer may be the most intelligent person in the room. But that doesn't mean that he has used his brains on his book. As Bobby Fischer put it after suffering one of his rare chess defeats, "It's one thing to be a good player and another thing to play well." It's one thing to have an IQ of 130, 150, or 170 and another thing to think. Even highly intelligent people have trouble with ideas and arguments, as evidenced by the fact that if you give a brilliant scientist a question outside of her/his field to answer, she/he will fumble about with her/his answer like any novice thinker.

When writers say that they don't like what they're writing, what they really mean is that they no longer like their own ideas and arguments. Seeing their ideas on the page, they no longer believe them. The second sentence undermines or contradicts the first. The point made in Chapter 1 is diluted or polluted in Chapter 4. The behavior of the main character no longer makes sense. The definitions of key words change so as to accommodate the writer's shifting ideas, but his central argument is weakened or killed in the process. In fiction and nonfiction, poetry and prose, articles and essays— wherever language is used—ideas and arguments are everything.

But instead of understanding that they're having trouble at the level of idea and argument, writers will say things like, "I'm having trouble with organization" or "I just can't work out the plot." We all have a hundred handy euphemisms to take our eye off the fact that we're having trouble thinking. So, to do a better job of keeping your eye on your ideas, refer to the following checklist with every piece you write:

1. What am I arguing for?
2. Is my argument convincing?
3. Do I believe it myself?
4. Am I consistent?
5. Am I clear?
6. Am I compelling?
7. Where is the argument strong?
8. Can I underline those strengths?
9. Where is the argument weak?
10. How can I strengthen it?

CRAFTING ANY ART

W. Joe Innis, a well-known and internationally collected painter with solo shows in Tokyo, Seoul, Buenos Aires, Istanbul, New York, and elsewhere, is also a novelist whose latest title is *Also Rising*. In the following piece he points out some basic connections between the craft of painting and the craft of prose.

The Muses of Writing and Painting

In my college years I read about discipline. Matter of fact, I read a lot about what writers had to say about what they did. This kind of reading fascinated me and, for a time, staved off the guilt that comes from not trying it myself. It also enabled me to dispel large chunks of this wisdom to my circle of friends and wannabe-writers. We all read these same books, but the advice bore repeating. This we did late at night over beers at a back table at The Keg, a proximate watering hole. Drinking is a good way to make you feel like an important writer.

Facing a typewriter is not. What we imagined under the influence of the suds—words welling out of us, intense periods lost to the muse, pages leaping from our Underwoods—became, after tedious hours of false starts, a single, heavily revised sentence that we would read and reread, hoping against hope that it would serve to catapult us deep into the Great American Novel. After college I worked as a journalist; and, since I still hadn't got many more than two consecutive pages toward my first novel done, I became a visual artist.

I stayed with this new profession long enough to learn something about color, line, and what light does to things, long enough to understand that, when a painting is going well, something I read in those books about writing happens to me. I do lose myself to the muse. Not all the time, certainly, but enough to count. And when I did, I found I was painting well over my head, a condition that can transform a journeyman into an artist.

> "And this is the way a novel gets written, in ignorance, fear, sorrow, madness, and a kind of psychotic happiness as an incubator for the wonders being born."
>
> —Jack Kerouac
>
> **Creativity and craft go together. Can you sense how?**

In fiction this kind of altered state of being is called "Letting the Book Write Itself." I remembered authors discussing the phenomenon in those books we read, how characters would take over the story and speak for themselves, and how the writer was reduced to the role of spectator. All he needed to do was get it down, no easy matter when it was coming thick and fast. They reported long hours working through the nights; too excited to sleep, they were up sometimes for days on end. It wasn't always literature that was happening to them, but if it wasn't, it was close.

In painting I've achieved this peculiar state regularly enough to expect it. When it doesn't come, I'm miffed. I struggle. Sometimes I wrestle the thing through, force it to behave. It's always a mistake. Ah, but when the spirit comes! So, if paintings came together like that for me, why not writing? Was this muse ready to embrace me as well?

By the time I returned for another try, Underwoods had given way to IBM Selectrics. Still, the words wouldn't come. The expectant hum of my type-writer was like an idling Buick, tremulous, potent, ready. Sometimes I had to shut it off. Sure, I was experiencing growing success in another medium, but with respect to my writing little more than my drinking habits had changed.

What there was to that success with a brush did permit me a little more latitude in judging myself. If the words didn't exactly gush forth, they did seep. I tried to convince myself that fluency was for the shallow. I was a slow writer. There were many of those, weren't there? But the word count was embarrassing. I was writing by accretion. At this rate, I'd have eighty thou-sand done about the time the lava flow beneath Hawaii's Big Island formed a land bridge to New Zealand.

What was so different about painting?

When I looked hard at the process of how I painted, I was in for a surprise. Paintings weren't completed as fast as I imagined; speed was an illusion. Starting a painting bore a heavy resemblance to the labors of writing. I'd forgotten the days I spent considering the subject I was to paint, what it meant to me, and how to best compose it and convey the meaning to others. I'd forgotten how much extraneous stuff had to be sifted through and dis-carded, the time it took to throttle emotions, to control oneself.

As a draftsman, I am hardly deft. My drawings would never be mistakenly archived with John Singer Sargent's or Bouguereau's. I fumble with sketches for days. Most—like my first attempts at writing something—are heavy-handed, hopeless. Burning is too good for them. The sketches done, the painting goes no better. I'd completely forgotten how I struggle to get the colors to vibrate, one against the other, how much of what I lay down is mistaken, how nothing works. It can be days before I find two colors that sing, the start of a painting.

So, the trouble with art was not a lot different from the trouble with writing. A painting—like writing—is a problem with too many solutions and not nearly enough rules. Things have to be thought about and got *through. A lot of things. Recognizing this enabled me to stay with the blank page. Staring at it or out the window is the creative process, too. That it takes time is unimportant. You won't be paid by the hour. You'll be lucky to be paid at all.*

What you're doing with all this seemingly unproductive time is convincing your muse you're serious. Once she believes you'll stay the course, that you want art more than life, she'll tiptoe up behind you, drape her lanky arms around your neck, and whisper in your ear. Go follow her anywhere.

FOOD FOR THOUGHT

"An author is one who can judge his own stuff's worth, without pity, and destroy most of it."—Colette
Can you judge your own stuff's worth?

"At least half the mystery novels published violate the law that the solution, once revealed, must seem to be inevitable."—Raymond Chandler
Do you understand what laws govern writing? Have you ever stopped to articulate them?

"A good rule for writers: do not explain overmuch."—W. Somerset Maugham
You've heard the phrase "Show, don't tell." Has it registered?

"Writers have no real area of expertise. They are merely generalists with a highly inflamed sense of punctuation."—Lorrie Moore
Do you love how language works, punctuation included?

"The mind loves images whose meaning is unknown, since the meaning of the mind is itself unknown."—René Magritte
How do you get both mystery and clarity into your writing?

"I might write four lines or I might write twenty. I subtract and I add until I really hit something. You don't always whittle down, sometimes you whittle up."—Grace Paley
Can you tell when more is needed?

"One of the great rules of art: do not linger."—André Gide
Can you tell when you need to get on with it?

*"Nothing is more odious than music without
hidden meanings."*—Frédéric Chopin
Is your writing full of hidden meanings?
Are you providing your readers with enough clues?

*"When the film is finished it is never the film
I said I wanted to make."*—Federico Fellini
Should a book look like its original idea? Or like itself?

*"All the worst things happen in the best works, and the worst music appears
to be streaked all through with the most luscious bits."*—Bernard Van Dieren
Do you accept that even a good piece can have its ups and downs?

*"I favor the picture which arrives at its destination without the evidence of a tiring
journey, rather than the one which shows the marks of battle."*—Charles Sheeler
Do you like your writing to be noticed or do you prefer that it get out of the way?

*"I start from something considered dead and arrive at a world.
And when I put a title on it, it becomes even more alive."*—Joan Miró
What do titles do?

*"No doubt, it is useful for an artist to know all the forms
of art which have preceded or which accompany his. But he
must be very careful not to look for models."*—Pablo Picasso
Do you often look for models? Are there times when following
a model makes sense? When it doesn't?

*"Every artist, from the moment he or she makes the first stroke
on canvas, is destined to follow a certain path."*—Perle Fine
As soon as you start a piece of writing, is its shape predetermined?
Or is there more flexibility than that?

*"Make the people live. Make them live. But my people must be more
than people. They must be an over-essence of people."*—John Steinbeck
Are you crafty enough to get at the essence of things?

4
A Writer's Personality

The psychologist Otto Rank has been called "the artist's psychologist" because of his interest in the contours of the creative personality. In *The Broken Image*, Clive Matson explained Rank's position:

> According to Rank, not many people are prepared to face the challenge of themselves, to assume full responsibility for their own existence. Rank concluded that there were three levels or styles of response to this self-challenge. The first, and most common, was simply to evade it; the second was to make an effort at self-encounter, only to fall back in confusion and defeat; the third, and much the least common, was that of carrying the confrontation through to self-acceptance and new birth.
>
> These three attitudes or approaches corresponded to Rank's three types of human character: the average or adapted type, content to swim adjustively and irresponsibly with the tide; the neurotic type, discontented both with civilization and with himself; and the creative type, as represented by the ideal types of the Artist and the Hero, at peace with himself and at one with others.

For Rank, creative people are those people who come to accept the responsibilities of freedom and will themselves to make meaning. If we wanted to give a simple definition of the writer's personality, we could do worse than the following twist on Rank's formulation: writers are people who live free, try to make sense of the world, and reject just fitting in. They are the people who are compelled to ask "Why?"—the ones who've embarked on a lifelong meaning-seeking odyssey. They write because it is meaningful to write, not because it is safe, easy, profitable, acceptable, reasonable, respectable, pleasurable, or commendable to write. They write in order to make manifest the freedom they are determined to champion.

At least, this is the picture of the ideal or idealized writer. Actual writers come in all shapes and sizes and are rather less heroic and less free than this ideal. They are enlivened by motives of all kinds, the inglorious as well as the glorious, and possess plenty of negative qualities along with the positive ones. They can be honorable or disloyal, empathic or self-centered, rebellious in healthy ways, crying out at injustice, blowing whistles when necessary, and charting their own course, or rebellious in unhealthy ways, fighting off good advice, burning their candles at both ends, and warding off intimacy. They are indeed heroic sometimes, and freer than most people, but they are first of all complex, contradictory, and unsettled human beings.

Let's begin our discussion of the personality issues of flesh-and-blood writers by taking a look at the following personality trait chart.

PERSONALITY TRAITS, THEIR EXCESSES, AND THEIR INSUFFICIENCIES

Take a look at the following list. On it are seventy-five personality traits culled from the creativity literature and from my work with creative and performing artists over the past fifteen years.

1. Access to emotions	26. Honesty
2. Alert to gaps in knowledge	27. Humanitarianism
3. Ambitiousness	28. Imagination
4. Anxiety tolerance	29. Ingenuity
5. Asks "Why?" questions	30. Intellectual honesty
6. Assertiveness	31. Intellectual playfulness
7. Breadth of knowledge	32. Intelligence
8. Compassion	33. Interest in challenges
9. Concentration	34. Interest in problems
10. Confidence	35. Interest in solutions
11. Convergent thinking abilities	36. Intrinsically motivated
12. Copes with novelty	37. Introspective stance
13. Courage	38. Intuition
14. Creativity	39. Love of beauty
15. Creativity in a domain	40. Love of complexity
16. Curiosity	41. Love of doubt
17. Decision-making capabilities	42. Love of freedom
18. Depth of knowledge	43. Love of goodness
19. Discipline	44. Love of language
20. Divergent thinking abilities	45. Love of logic
21. Empathy	46. Love of mystery
22. Energy	47. Love of simplicity
23. Evaluative abilities	48. Metaphoric thinking abilities
24. Existential outlook	49. Moral outlook
25. Flexibility	50. Nonconformity

51. Openness to experience
52. Optimism
53. Originality
54. Passion
55. Patience
56. Persistence
57. Playfulness
58. Pleasure capabilities
59. Questions norms/assumptions
60. Reality-testing abilities
61. Resiliency
62. Risk-taking orientation
63. Self-centeredness
64. Self-direction
65. Self-trust
66. Sense of humor
67. Sensitivity
68. Seriousness
69. Skepticism
70. Spiritual outlook
71. Thoughtfulness
72. Tolerance
73. Tolerance for ambiguity
74. Unconcern with social approval
75. Uses knowledge base

The person who sufficiently manifests these seventy-five traits is equipped to write. To write is to be sufficiently passionate, self-trusting, assertive, thoughtful, skeptical, and all the rest. But to be creative *and* mentally healthy is to be all of these things in just the right way—to be passionate but not too wild, self-trusting but not too grandiose, thoughtful but not too obsessional, skeptical but not too nihilistic. Working writers are in regular danger of "going too far" with respect to each trait. One of their prime tasks is to moderate their excesses.

Conversely, the would-be writer or the blocked writer is more likely to manifest insufficiencies. He is not self-directing enough, doesn't tolerate ambiguity well enough, and so on. The challenge for this person is to manifest "more" of the qualities in question—not just in order to write, but because the ideal of mental health involves being sufficiently passionate, self-trusting, empathic, curious, playful, thoughtful, and so on.

Strive to manifest all of these qualities in just the right proportions. If you do that, you will be a lifelong writer and as mentally healthy as a person can be.

THE INNER LIFE OF THE WRITER

To say that a writer is basically introspective or that she requires solitude in order to think her thoughts hardly catches the flavor of her riotous inner life. What defines the writer more than anything else is her rich, roiling, sometimes light but often dark inner busyness, a busyness made up of daydreams, worries, thought fragments, and elaborated thoughts, an inner reality filled with the music she has heard and still dwells upon, the sights she has seen

> *"Fortunately I have never developed any real idiosyncrasies, such as turning squashed frogs into frisbees, writing fan letters to soap-opera stars, or eating organic food. I am, on that score, quite normal."*
>
> —David Gilhooly
>
> **What is "normal" for a writer? What is "abnormal"?**

and still dwells upon, the sentences that form and dissolve and form again, finally becoming the opening paragraph of a book she had no idea she was intending to write.

All of the words of a certain sort that we use to characterize writers—observer, witness, thinker, dreamer, outsider—speak to the primary importance of this inner activity in a writer's life. A writer's inner life matters: it is hard to imagine that anything matters more. Nor is this inner life something that anyone else is privy to, unless and until the writer wants to share it. It is a private, secret hotbed of activity, an unruly, unquiet, unholy cauldron bubbling with the best and the worst thoughts a person can think. It is a place where the writer destroys the world, just to see what might be left; where she tries out her seductions and revenges; where she remeets her transformed parents, who now look like characters in a novel, and presents them with a crisis that tests them and ruins them.

Part of this inner activity is the writer creating. She is dreaming her characters, spinning her tales, following the path of her plots. She is also remembering the look of the boarding school in which she was placed when she was six, the smell of the farm she left when she was seventeen. She is also making herself miserable as she feels again, "only" in her mind but no less painfully for that, the wounds inflicted upon her by the betrayals, failures, and shortcomings of others; and by her own self-betrayals, failures, and shortcomings. She is likewise fantasizing about her bestsellers, her sexual escapades, her high adventures and heroic misdemeanors. Hours and hours of her day are spent doing all this "nothing." She doesn't move; all you can see is her expression changing.

You might say, "Of course my inner life is like that! But isn't everyone's?" The answer is yes and no; and more no than yes. The typical person does not permit herself all that dream time. Her basic orientation is away from her own thoughts; she is bound to worry a lot and daydream some, like all human beings, she is bound to occasionally hear inner music and occasionally revisit inner sights, like all human beings, but her orientation is away from that reflective way of being, that dancing with language, that constant questioning and wondering, which characterizes writers and other creative people.

The typical person would rather watch television than tell herself a story. The typical person would rather read a book than write one. The typical person feels safer keeping dangerous thoughts at arm's length rather than looking at them squarely, and so is surprised to learn that there is no love in her marriage, that her smiling uncle is a drunken batterer, or that the dogma of her religion makes no sense whatsoever. In short, the typical person feels unfriendly toward ideas and what the mind can do, while the writer—and every other creative person—can't live unless she honors her inner reality.

Because of this need, each writer is inhabited by a vast, roiling, secret inner world in which much less is resolved than the writer's outer appearance might lead us to believe. The writer is something of a shape-changer and trickster, someone a little more treacherous, eccentric, and unpredictable than she at first appears, because she is continually buffeted and transformed by an inner life invisible from the outside. She may speak to her mate in complete sentences about what her day was like, but inside another life is being lived, one full of beauties and monstrosities, upheavals and transgressions. Even if the writer safely contains that inner reality—sublimates her urges, controls her thoughts, manages her monsters—it nevertheless remains alive inside of her, always ready to produce the next book or sorrow, the next meaning spark or meaning crisis.

So:

1. Relish your inner life.
2. Watch out. Inside your mind are the good, the bad, and the ugly.

Q & A

I think I have an obsessive-compulsive personality. Is that true of many writers? Should I try to do something about it? Will that be a big problem in my life?

Yes, yes, and yes.

Many writers have what look to be obsessive-compulsive personalities. But what does this mean exactly? Is it something about brain wiring and heredity? Does it have more to do with anxiety? Or is it just a heightened interest in what one's interested in? Think of a young child building something. He might work for hours, minutely obsessing about the way his castle is shaping up. Is this a problem and a sign of illness? In some cases it

> *"I am one individual, imprisoned in myself, hanged and condemned to solitary in my own ego for life."*
>
> —Jean Tinguely

Is personality like a straitjacket? What would it mean to shed it? What would you gain and what would you lose?

might be, but in most cases it isn't. In most cases it's just a sign that the child has permission from himself and from his parents to learn through doing: permission to experiment, permission to be a child.

But another child who obsesses in this way may indeed be having emotional problems and blocking them out by focusing intently on his building project. This child obsesses not because building is so intrinsically fascinating but because he's trying to avoid the painful thoughts and feelings that are just out of conscious awareness. If this child's house is toppled over, he may scream and throw a fit out of all proportion to the loss. The first child loves building; the second child is defending himself through building.

Still, in real life, real children manifest a mixture of motivations. Some of their obsessiveness will be healthy and fine and some of it will reflect emotional issues seething underneath. That's why it's so hard to distinguish between "positive" obsessiveness and "negative" obsessiveness. The same is true later in life. Why does a painter like Van Gogh obsess for a lifetime about the color blue, so familiarizing himself with its resonances that he can paint irises or night skies that stand for the ages? Part of his obsession with color must have been rooted in the fact that we are built to love and respond to color: color speaks to us. In that regard, his obsession was altogether positive. But part of his obsession must have related to thoughts and feelings about his cold parents, the son he left, his failed career as a preacher, his lack of recognition, and other painful matters that could be kept at bay just so long as he obsessed about color.

Writers' obsessions and compulsions are a similar mixed bag. To want to begin a new book the moment your current book is finished may mean that you are brimming over with ideas and can't stand the thought of wasting precious time, but it may also mean that you are afraid of the existential depression that is likely to hit if you stop working for even a second. Because of these complexities, it isn't reasonable to argue that a writer shouldn't obsess and shouldn't act compulsively. But we can reasonably propose the following:

1. If you feel out of control or the pain is too severe, you've gone too far. Whatever is going on underneath must be addressed. The tail is wagging the dog. Look into supportive psychotherapy and the pharmaceutical treatment of OCD (Obsessive-Compulsive Disorder). Get help and pledge to make some changes.

2. If your relationships with your mate, your children, and other intimates suffer because of your obsessions and compulsions, that makes them suspect. If you can never calmly chat with your child because your mind is always teeming and racing, that is a problem.

3. Obsessions and compulsions are often rooted in and fueled by our anxieties. Learn to manage anxiety better. Learn what stress reduction techniques work for you. Then use them.

ADDICTIONS

Genetics and upbringing aside, writers will incline in the direction of addictions for one, some, or all of the following reasons:

* For existential reasons, having to do with the need to do something or anything with the empty, meaningless time between creative efforts, coupled, for the blocked or underutilized artist, with having too much time of that sort on his hands.

* For personality reasons, connected to a need to rebel, a greediness for experience, a risk-taking attitude, an asocial stance, a curiosity about this or that substance or sexual experience, etc. (Look back at the personality trait chart and think about the shadow side of the traits listed there.)

* For mood-altering reasons, having to do with the need to manage or fend off the persistent, even lifelong, low-grade depression that comes with high intelligence, good reality-testing, and the postmodern condition.

* For mind-altering reasons, having to do with the pull to take a break from brooding introspection, the tension of ideas, and the chatter of negative self-talk among other problematic issues related to being a writer.

> *"I hate television. I hate it as much as peanuts. But I can't stop eating peanuts."*
> —Orson Welles
>
> **To what things are you addicted?**

* For anxiety-management reasons, having to do with binding normal, neurotic, existential, and artistic anxiety, including anxieties associated with current creative projects.
* For identity reasons, connected to identification with outsiders, rebels, misfits, "freaks," "low lifes," "wild ones," or "artistic types."
* For escape and avoidance reasons, so as to avoid the demands of freedom, the taxing nature of creative work, the pain of career lows, and persistent negative feelings.
* For self-soothing reasons, to give oneself a treat—a high, an orgasm, a rush, a thrill—in the midst of a practically difficult and existentially gloomy life.
* For reasons having to do with the (misguided) idea that a drug-induced state is a freer, better, more imaginative, more creative state than a "straight mind" state.
* For "damping down" reasons having to do with managing an excess of energy—that is, with the need to somehow control and handle a large life force.

For these reasons, many writers fall prey to addictions. As Tom Dardis explained in *The Thirsty Muse*:

> *Of the seven [now eight] native-born Americans awarded the Nobel Prize in literature, five were alcoholic. The list of other twentieth-century Americans writers similarly afflicted is very long; only a few of the major talents have been spared. In addition to the five Nobel laureates—Sinclair Lewis, Eugene O'Neill, William Faulkner, Ernest Hemingway and John Steinbeck—the roster includes Edward Arlington Robinson, Jack London, Edna St. Vincent Millay, F. Scott Fitzgerald, Hart Crane, Conrad Aiken, Thomas Wolfe, Dashiell Hammett, Dorothy Parker, Ring Lardner, Djuna Barnes, John O'Hara, James Gould Cozzens, Tennessee Williams, John Berryman, Carson McCullers, James Jones, John Cheever, Jean Stafford, Truman Capote, Raymond Carver, Robert Lowell and James Agee. A closer look at the long list of alcoholic writers reveals that four were suicides (Jack London, Hart Crane, Hemingway and John Berryman), while nearly all the rest burned themselves out at surprisingly early stages of their careers.*

A well-known novelist missed her first appointment with me because, on the day before the appointment and while intoxicated, she fell down a flight of stairs, broke her hip, and landed in the hospital. Within a year her drinking had killed her. Other clients have gone on ruinous binges, flown into session on speed, sold their computers for drug money. One client, a poet, lived only for pain killers, while another, a screenwriter, likened his obsession with speed to "a Chinese water torture." A third lived his isolated, claustrophobic life always high on marijuana. Some were hooked on sex chats on the Internet and other up-to-the-minute addictions.

Addiction has real biological and psychological components, but at root it is probably a meaning problem. Therefore, while it can afflict anyone, it is that much more likely to afflict writers, who are perpetually troubled by meaning drains, meaning voids, and other powerful meaning crises. Colin Wilson, chronicling Lord Byron's love affairs with married women and young boys during the winter of 1818, explained: "Byron's chief problem was a simple one: *he had no idea what to do with himself.* He knew he found social life boring and dissatisfying, but what was the alternative? Life became an endless flight from boredom, rolling in his carriage around Europe and making a virtue of his fatigue by complaining about it in his poems."

Once having taken root, an addiction reduces a person's freedom to make personal meaning while increasing psychological and physical dependence on the thing craved. The addiction begins to take care of meaning crises in its own way, producing a satisfactory and even a happy bondage. The great irony about addiction is that, despite its nasty consequences, despite the guilt and despair that come from knowing that one is out of control, the addiction is still less of a problem than is freedom. The bondage is real bondage but almost a happy bondage, for while addicted there is no question about how to fill up one's time. You drink and drink and drink (and sleep it off, get sick, go to the hospital, make scenes, lose friends, break bones, and so forth). This, it turns out, is easier than asking and answering the question, "What am I to going do with my freedom?"

There is a beautiful story in the existential tradition, "The Bound Man" by the German author Ilse Aichinger. In its setting and tone, it is like Kafka's "The Hunger Artist." A man awakens one morning to find himself inexplicably bound by rope, but instead of removing the rope at the first opportunity he decides to become a circus attraction. The addict, also inexplicably bound to his or her addiction, has, like the bound man, important reasons not to fight it, for while he is bound up with it he is less free but also less anxious. Bound this way, there are so many things one can't even dream of doing, so many powerful limitations—which restriction is experienced as liberation!

Linda Schierse Leonard, examining her own alcoholism and her thoughts on the relationship between addiction and creativity in *Witness to the Fire: Creativity and the Veil of Addiction*, explained:

> *When I looked up the word addiction in the dictionary, I found a connection between addiction and creativity buried in the original etymological roots. The Latin for addict, addictus, means to devote, surrender, deliver over, or give oneself up habitually. Is addiction, then, the act of giving oneself over to something as one's master—be it a substance, object, person,*

or activity—*so totally that one's entire being and meaning become possessed by it? This sense of being possessed corresponded to my experience as an addict. Some of the things we give ourselves over to in this way are alcohol, drugs, food, cigarettes, gambling, shopping, romance, sex, work, money, power, and control. None of these things are bad in and of themselves. But if one is possessed by them, if one gives up one's whole being to something else, allowing oneself to be ruled by something external, one's freedom and personal integrity are lost. In this kind of giving up or delivering oneself over, one loses one's soul.*

What is an addict to do? Something. If he goes to the right therapist, that may be a great something. One human being will meet and encounter another. Joining will begin. The therapist will create chinks in the client's wall of denial, pointing out contradictions, probing, disputing, reality-testing, confronting, educating. The therapist will assert that the addiction is a hindrance to healthy living and help the client see just how much freedom has been lost. With luck, the client will agree that this all-too-happy bondage must end. Then recovery, punctuated by slips, cravings, and disasters, can begin.

IDENTITY TROUBLES

It has surprised me to learn how important "identity issues" turn out to be in the lives of writers. Often the primary concern a writer brings to therapy has to do with some basic question about who he or she *really* is.

> "There are so many selves in everybody and to explore and exploit just one is wrong, dead wrong, for the creative person."
>
> —James Dickey
>
> Are you made up of many selves or have you an essential self? If you have an essential self, what's it like?

But "identity" is as challenging a concept as any that confronts us. For instance, we have no idea why one person is homosexual, another heterosexual, and a third bisexual. Nor do we know whether there is a primary "female identity" and a primary "male identity" that would show themselves if all cultural and historical particulars were wiped away. Nor do we know whether, when we say that this man has a strong "feminine" side or that woman a strong "masculine" side, we are talking about psychology or about biology. Nor do we know how to distinguish between the "identity a person is born with" and the "identity a person acquires." These are just a few of things that we do not know.

Why, for instance, are so many writers bisexual? To put the matter the other way around, why are so many bisexuals creative? Can a woman only be creative if she is also "masculine"? Can a man only be creative if he is also "feminine"? Are creativity and bisexuality somehow linked, and if so, how? Is the linkage in the area of unhealthy narcissism: that the writer and the bisexual are both terrifically self-obsessed? Is the linkage positive rather than negative: that the sensitive, rebellious, intelligent person will be drawn to one of the arts and also drawn to all people, male or female, who share a certain sensitivity, rebelliousness, and intelligence? It is fair to say that we do not know the answers and hardly know how to frame the questions.

Nor are these speculations merely intellectual food for thought. These issues matter in the lives of a real flesh-and-blood writers. For instance, many of the male writers I see make love to women, live with them, and marry them, but also obsess and fantasize about sex with men. Is there a primary heterosexual identity in these men which has become distorted, or a primary homosexual identity which is making itself felt through these obsessions? Or is what we're seeing a kind of unsettled identity made up of multiple biological urges and shifting psychological and cultural factors?

Let me ground these observations with some concrete examples. I'm thinking of three clients: I'll call them Tom the poet, Dick the screenwriter, and Harry the playwright.

Tom, who is in his early twenties, has a gay brother. Dick, in his early forties, has a straight brother and a straight sister. Harry, who is nearing fifty, has one gay brother and one straight brother. Each is accepting of the sexual orientation of others—none is anti-gay—but each feels revulsion at his own homosexual impulses and actions. Each rejects the idea that he is latently homosexual or even bisexual. Rather, each harbors the virtually identical feeling that his obsession is not really about sexual orientation, sexual identity, or even about sex per se, but about something else. That "something else" is very hard to pin down, but it has to do with going to "an edge" of some sort: with falling over that edge into danger or else with withdrawing from that edge to the not fully desirable safety of heterosexuality. A naked man's chest is more than an object of desire for these men: it is a challenge, a totem, both attractive and repulsive, inviting and threatening, beautiful and horrible.

Tom the poet says that men better mirror him than do women. For him, men are "full" while women are "empty." He flirts with men, takes walks with men, talks art with men. But sleeping with men fills him with revulsion—though he is about to take that plunge.

Dick the screenwriter acts compulsively, reaching out for men in dark places, and then feels stupid afterward. Back in the daylight, he shamefacedly dodges the fellows with whom he's spent a few seconds and worries about the honesty and integrity of his new marriage.

Harry, for his part, so far has had no flings with men. He considers that too dangerous, something from which he might not recover. But he, like the others, is obsessed, waking and sleeping, by images of men. He is aware of the men around him wherever he goes—in bookstores, in restaurants, at the movies—making even the purchase of a magazine a hellish adventure. Still, he remains convinced that the answer doesn't lie in the direction of dating men, because, not insignificantly, actual men do not interest him. Men in his dreams torment him and entice him; men everywhere affect him; but actual men, once he singles them out and speaks to them, he can take or leave.

There are psychological theories about all of this, having to do with faulty childhood development, intrapsychic conflicts, psychological inversions, sado-masochistic impulses, love objects gone awry, and so forth. There are social and political theories, about androgyny, about the cultural concomitants of manhood and womanhood, about the virtues of possessing both sensitivity and instrumentality. And there are biological theories as well, about hormonal baths *in utero* and genetic predispositions. There are many, many ways to look at this. But the riddle remains. We simply do not know the answer.

Some of you are thinking, "Don't be naive, my friend, these men are just gay—and in denial!" Others of you may be thinking, "These are just narcissistic and indiscriminately lustful guys—like lots of other guys!" But I think we simply don't know. The hypotheses we might come up with are plentiful enough. But they are hypotheses, not answers. Even after we generate our intelligent list of hypotheses, the riddle remains. Why lust after that which revolts you? What does "identity" mean, if it can include terrors like this? Paul Gauguin commented late in life, "The problem one seeks to solve is easy at the beginning and a sphinx at death." What these conflicts represent remains a genuine riddle.

Identity issues are of profound importance in the lives of human beings. If I dream of being something—say, "creative"—and think that I am something else—say, "uncreative"—that is an important identity problem. If I think that I am something—say, "a novelist"—but also think that I am limited in some way—say, with regard to my ability to plot or write dialogue—that, it turns out, is also an identity problem. Every single adjective I use by way of self-identification—bold, timid, smart, stupid, Irish, Mexican, Catholic, Buddhist, mother, childless—is an identity conflict-in-the-making.

But whereas people regularly report that they are depressed or blocked, they do not announce that they have an identity problem. It is in the nature of identity problems that, if we are to recognize their effects in our life, we have to become attuned to their presence. We can hear their insidious presence in each of the following statements:

* ✳ "I'm a pretty accomplished novelist, but my dad still hopes that I'll change my mind and become a chemist."
* ✳ "I'm a serious writer, but the culture seems to want entertainers only."
* ✳ "I think like a writer, but I haven't the discipline to sit down, stay put, and actually write."
* ✳ "I want to write, but when I plant myself in front of a blank screen something like performance anxiety derails me."
* ✳ "I can't sell my writing because I'm incredibly shy."
* ✳ "What kind of writing is a good Christian permitted to do?"
* ✳ "I'd love to write children's books, but I'm just too uncreative."
* ✳ "I'm a Catholic writer in a Protestant country."
* ✳ "I just can't see spending a whole year on a book that might fail."

Identity is a massive, complicated, mysterious subject. The typical introductory psychology text simply omits the word "identity" from its index and avoids the matter entirely. Erik Erikson, whom we associate with the concept of "identity," could himself only acknowledge how complex an answer is required of the superficially simple question, "What is my identity?" He explained: "I can attempt to make the subject matter of identity more explicit only by approaching it from a variety of angles. At one time it will appear to refer to a *conscious sense of individual identity*; at another to an unconscious striving for a *continuity of personal character*; at a third, to the silent doings of *ego synthesis*; and, finally, as a maintenance of an inner *solidarity* with a group's ideals and identity." Nor does this "finally" really mean finally, for Erikson, as any of us would in his shoes, continued to add meanings and make further distinctions as he explored his subject.

The point to remember is this. "Identity" is more than dynamic: it is a wild thing, made up, as often as not, of parts that contradict one another and parts that make war on one another. The "identity" of the typical writer is wilder still, more unsettled, more raucous, more internally at odds. Just to be able to articulate these disputes can be a great boon, even if no way to smooth away contradictions or resolve internal conflicts immediately suggests itself. For a writer, this very articulation may prove to be the starting point for a literary adventure and a spurt of growth and healing.

DEPRESSION

Writers are prone to depression. Among some of the better-known writers to have experienced severe depression are Hans Christian Anderson, Honoré de Balzac, Charles Baudelaire, William Blake, Lord Byron, Emily Dickinson, Charles Dickens, T. S. Eliot, Ralph Waldo Emerson, William Faulkner, F. Scott Fitzgerald, Nikolai Gogol, Graham Greene, Herman Hesse, Victor Hugo, Henrik Ibsen, John Keats, Robert Lowell, Herman Melville, Boris Pasternak, Sylvia Plath, Alexander Pushkin, Mary Shelley, Robert Louis Stevenson, Dylan Thomas, Leo Tolstoy, Mark Twain, Tennessee Williams, and Mary Wollstonecraft (according to Kay Jamison in *Touched with Fire*, her book on creativity and bipolar disorder).

But it isn't just the impressive magnitude of this list, the suicides of well-known writers like Ernest Hemingway and Virginia Woolf, and the memoirs of writers like William Styron that drive this point home. So do the anecdotal reports of hundreds of everyday writers (and their therapists) and so do the many research studies that have been conducted on the subject, both here and abroad. The message is clear: writers are significantly more prone to depression than are members of the general population. In fact, it may be impossible to be a writer and avoid at least periodic bouts of depression.Constance Holden wrote in the April 1987 issue of *Psychology Today*:

> *"The world I create in writing compensates for what the real world does not give me."*
> —Gloria Anzaldua
>
> **What does the real world fail to give you?**

In the early 1970s, Nancy Andreasen of the University of Iowa College of Medicine completed a study of fifteen topflight American writers at the prestigious University of Iowa Writers' Workshop and compared them with others matched for age, education and sex. Ten of the writers had histories of mood disorders, compared with only two from the comparison group. Andreasen has continued the study during the past fifteen years, expanding the sample of writers to thirty. According to a recent report, the proportion of writers treated for mood disorders has increased to 80%, compared to 30% of the comparison group [and] 43% of the writers had some degree of manic-depressive illness, as compared to 10% of the others. Two of the thirty committed suicide during the fifteen years of the study.

As to why depression among writers should be so prevalent, one can hazard some reasonable guesses. The personality of the writer, rooted in the sort of self-relationship that demands that she know things for herself and that she speak in her own voice, is naturally also the kind of personality that will be prone to meaning lapses, boredom, and existential depression. Second, the writer's work can be depressingly hard to do. Once in a while a piece comes out whole and reads well from beginning to end; but more often than not it is a prolonged, agonizing struggle to get from nothing to something, to make the journey from fleeting idea to accomplished novel or play. Third, if you write things that you cannot sell, that is a depressing problem. The writer is looking depression squarely in the eye because of her own personality, the work she does, the nature of the world in which she is embedded, and the nature of the marketplace with which she must deal.

Usually clinicians say that depressions are biopsychosocial in nature. What we mean is that since we can't really pin down a depression's root causes, we had better implicate everything we can thing of, from genetics to traffic jams, from childhood trauma to neural transmission problems, from a lack of social support to low self-esteem. Intrapsychic conflicts with regard to self-worth, a fear of negative evaluations and a loss of self-esteem at the hands of critics, an inability to handle the stresses of independent decision-making, the consequences of alcohol and drug use, an inability to do the writing of one's dreams, real or perceived skill deficits, deadline pressure, alienation from the general culture, and the relentless pressure of day jobs all can and do bring on bouts of depression. There is a bewildering list of potential and actual causes complicating and implicated in any particular case of depression.

But it seems to me that a lot of the depression writers experience has to do with meaning drains and meaning losses. We regularly lose our reasons for living. Because a writer has seen through to the fact that there is no ultimate meaning and that all meanings are personal and transient, she may put on a good face and continue to invest meaning in her writing, but she is making this effort against a background of real meaninglessness. This background reality has the power to come forward at any moment and produce a serious existential depression.

Is there any treatment or cure for *this* kind of depression? Let's wend our way toward an answer.

ROLE PLAY:
A Depressed Writer Visits the Zoo

Person A:. You are a quite depressed writer who has gotten up the energy to take your eleven-year-old nephew/niece to the zoo. You like this child very much and you will try your best to listen to him/her and answer any questions he/she poses. (If you've had no experience with depression, this may be a difficult role to play. But since most writers become depressed now and then, both as a constitutional matter and as a result of the practical difficulties of the writing life, I am guessing that you will have enough experience with depression to step into these shoes.)

Person B: You are an eleven-year-old boy or girl on an outing with your writer aunt or uncle. You see that he/she is very sad and you wonder why this is so. Ask as many questions as it takes until you think you really understand why he/she is sad. Then see if you can get him/her to provide you with some solutions, some best guesses as to what might help, or just some baby steps he/she can imagine taking to feel a little better. Be a wise, innocent eleven-year-old therapist and remember, you would really like your uncle/aunt to feel better.

Debriefing Questions

Questions for the writer to answer:

1. What was the experience like for you?
2. What did it feel like to act "depressed"? What did you notice about your body? Your mind? Your outlook?
3. Did you sense that you might be able to shake a depressive episode by talking with another human being?
4. If talking didn't seem to help, why do you think it proved ineffective? Primarily because talking can't change the basic "facts of existence"?
5. If depression can't be entirely eradicated, how can it be reduced or—as odd as this sounds—embraced?

Questions for the nephew/niece to answer:

1. What was the experience like for you?
2. Did the writer seem to have a clear idea or only hazy ideas about the sources or causes of his/her depression?
3. Did it seem to help to bring his/her sadness out into the open?
4. What about the writer's depression seemed most open to change? What seemed least open?

5. Did you feel "infected" by his/her sadness? Or did your "therapeutic stance" provide a buffer?

Questions for the observers to answer:

1. What especially struck you about the interaction?
2. What could you identify as the sources or causes of the writer's depression?
3. As a group, how many different kinds of writer's depressions can you identify? Which seem to have to do with personality and which with biology? Which seem to have to do with the writer's work? Which seem to have to do with the writer's world (including this culture and this marketplace)?
4. What would help to lift a writer's depression? If that seems to depend on the nature or cause of the depression, provide a remedy for each different kind of depression.
5. What helps with your own depressions?

MAKING CHOICES

You are depressed. Do you:

    (a) Ignore it?
    (b) Take something for it?
    (c) Do something to shake it?
    (d) Get laid up by it?
    (e) Write anyway?

The answer is: all of the above. It would be nice if there were a pill or an herb to ingest to relieve depression, but depression is only sometimes a phenomenon that can be cured by taking something. Sometimes—an awful lot of the time—it is a psychological reaction to life. If your day job is getting you down and prevents you from writing, if this goes on year after year, who wouldn't gain weight, grow irritable, or start to self-destruct? If your writing is rejected for a decade straight and you haven't been in love for even longer than that, who wouldn't feel like sleeping twenty-four hours a day or killing the first person who smiles?

Depression is with us. At this moment in the evolution of the species depression is especially with us, because we seriously doubt that the universe is anything but silent and indifferent. Existential depression is epidemic. It is also the case that the personality of the writer is a medium that grows depression beautifully. The same qualities that make writers self-directing, empathic, passionate, thoughtful, truthful, nonconforming, and all the rest produce people wide open to psychological depression. In addition, the work we do as writers, as draining and difficult as that can be, produces its own stresses, and so does the world in which we live, a world full of bestsellers that make us sad and envious and also full of repeated criticism and rejection. The writer's road leads right to depression.

If a writer's depression were strictly biological, it would be sensible to talk about doing something pharmaceutical or nutritional for it whenever a bout hit. You would take your Prozac or St. John's Wort and get better. But because depression comes to writers for reasons that can't be just biological, the truth is that we can't avoid the pain of depression or easily stop a bout once it hits. Sometimes it will lay us up and we will just be blue baggage on the bed, inert and despairing. If it is a low-grade depression, we may be able to ignore it and go about our business, writing, finding little pleasures, living. But often—too often—the depression will be severer than that and we won't be able to ignore it.

Clearly we should do as many sensible things as possible to rid our-selves of the depressions that we can't ignore. If the depression looks to be connected to childhood trauma, ongoing psychological conflicts, issues like self-revulsion or unreleased anger, and so on, then psychotherapy, in conjunction with drug therapy, may be the wisest course to pursue. This can help. If the depression looks to be connected to your cocaine use and your dangerous, out-of-control life, then dealing with the addiction must come first. If the depression looks to be about your failures in the market-place, then rethinking your business tactics and determining to meet the marketplace differently, or else finding a new love to devote your heart and mind to, are vital, immediate tasks.

It is possible to gain a repertoire of things to do to help shake off a depression, things both small and large, simple and complex—getting some sunshine, embarking on an adventure, running a few miles, taking a steamy shower, talking to a therapist, falling in love, releasing hurts and anger, eat-ing well, reinvesting in and reinventing meaning. Gaining such a repertoire is wise and helpful, because for many writers the curse of depression will always be just a small crisis away, lurking there, ready to pounce. Three out of four days you may be able to handle it with a walk on the beach and a butterscotch sundae, but that fourth day you may get right to your wits' end. It would be pretty to think that full cures are available; but depression is probably a prominent, unavoidable feature of modern life, only a "dis-ease" if we want to call modern life itself diseased and unbearable.

FOOD FOR THOUGHT

*"The creative person is both more primitive and more
cultivated than the average person."*—Frank Barron

In what sense are you more primitive than the average person? In what sense are you
more cultivated? Are these qualities opposed, complementary, or something else?

*"Every man carries in himself the germs of every human quality, and
sometimes one manifests itself, and sometimes another, and the man often
becomes unlike himself, while still remaining the same man."*—Leo Tolstoy

How have you become unlike yourself? Have you become an addict,
a depressive, even a monster, even though that isn't really you?
What will you do to become you again?

*"If a character is brutal, it is because I am brutal.
I take the blame and the credit."*—Maria Irene Fornes

What in your personality is reflected in your writing?

*"You never paint what you see or think you see. You paint with
a thousand vibrations the blow that struck you."*—Nicholas de Stael

What blows have you received that you must write about?

*"I have made it appear as though my motives were wholly public-spirited.
I don't want to leave that as my final impression. All writers are vain, selfish
and lazy, and at the very bottom of their motives lies a mystery."*—George Orwell

Are you vain, selfish, and lazy? Are you too vain, selfish, and lazy?

"It's in the ability to deceive oneself that the greatest talent is shown."—Anatole France

All writers are good liars. What are you lying to yourself about that you should admit?

*"The best thoughts you have are when you're young, and the
best you can do is never give up those thoughts."*—Rockwell Kent

What are the thoughts from childhood that you are still working and reworking?

*"Art plainly calls for both feeling and reasoning. In support of this assertion the
familiar example of Johann Sebastian Bach may be credited: mathematical and
theological books stood side by side on the shelves of his library."*—Max Bill

Are you equally adept at feeling and reasoning? Should you be?

"Artists are so vulnerable that, despite their tough exterior, they are influenced by trivia that they would consciously reject."—Edward Ruscha
Are you so vulnerable and anxious that "trivia" regularly derail you? What can you do about that?

"The quality which makes a man want to write and be read is essentially a desire for self-exposure and is masochistic. Like one of those guys who has a compulsion to take his thing out and show it on the street."—James Jones
Is your desire to write rooted in exhibitionism? Only to a small extent? To too great an extent?

"The writer should never be ashamed of staring. There is nothing that does not require his attention."—Flannery O'Connor
Is staring an essential part of your personality?

"Beyond all purist preconceptions, fantastic, aesthetic, or theoretical, is the imperious necessity to shout, to express oneself as one is."—Antonio Saura
Are you willing to shout? Are you able to shout?

"Most people pass out of the make-believe stage of childhood, but I'm still in it. I don't think you can act without one foot in the pram."—Derek Jacobi
How can you nurture or reclaim the "child-like" part of your personality?

"I suppose I am a born novelist, for the things I imagine are more vital and vivid to me than the things I remember."—Ellen Glasgow
Are you forever imagining? Is that central to your personality?

"As before, there is a great silence, with no end in sight. The writer surrenders, listening."—Jayne Anne Phillips
Listen to your own personality. What do you hear?

5
A Writer's Challenges

The writer's own personality is challenging. So is the work he does. So is the task of selling his work. Where to begin? Let's start off with a writer's perennial challenge: dealing with criticism and rejection.

CRITICISM, REJECTION, AND THE OPINION OF OTHERS

Some years ago I received word that I'd come in second in a prestigious national novel-writing competition. Coming in second in a national novel-writing competition is like coming in second in major league sports. You're a loser. Of course, you don't have to feel like a loser. You can say to yourself, "I came so far" or "I came *this* close." You can say, "What do *they* know?" You can say, "Did I really enter *that* contest?" But still, when all is said and done, in this America of ours, second place makes you a loser.

Actually I was busy with other things by the time of the announcement and didn't much notice the rejection. After the first hundred rejections that come in a writer's life, each subsequent one is easier to ignore; except, of course, those that really matter or that somehow get under the skin. This wasn't one of those—for one thing, the rejection letter was gentle and flattering—and I didn't give it much thought. I prepared to put the manuscript away until I could think of a new place to send it.

> *"I went for years not finishing anything. Because, of course, when you finish something you can be judged."*
>
> —Erica Jong
>
> **Are you ready to be judged? Are you ready for a lifetime of judgments, criticisms, and rejections?**

But as I went to put the manuscript away, I noticed that the readers' comments had been accidentally included. Here was a moment of truth! Did I dare read them? Did I want some "objective feedback"? Did I want some hurt feelings? I went ahead and read them. One note said, in an intelligent and carefully crafted paragraph, that the novel I'd submitted was among the best things the reader had ever read. The other said, in an equally intelligent and carefully crafted paragraph, that the novel was among the worst things the reader had ever read.

Isn't this a lesson that we have to learn again and again, that every opinion is an assertion of personality? That every belief is a fragment of autobiography? There was a book I once read that contained nothing but reviews of E. M. Forster's *A Passage to India*. To say that there was a range of opinion hardly captures the absolutely mind-boggling diversity of opinion expressed in those reviews. Brilliant and boring, humane and inhuman, slow and gripping, crystalline and impenetrable: there was nothing under the sun that wasn't said about that novel! Each reviewer had an agenda, not necessarily with Forster, but just with life.

I noticed the other day in the library, while reading some book reviews in a data bank, that each book review came with a letter grade. I looked up a well-known novelist's most recent novel and saw exactly what I expected to see: five reviews, five different grades. Her new novel had received an A, B, C, D, and F. Of course! I looked up a review of one of my own books, the *Variety* review of *Staying Sane in the Arts*. Someone had given it a B.

Another second place!

In this culture of winning and losing, the criticism we receive is that much more painful because we ourselves are rankers. The poet Theodore Roethke once ran into the house of a fellow poet (was it Robert Lowell?) and exclaimed, "I believe that right now I am the number one poet in America, you are number two, and 'x' is number three!" We may fervently wish to eradicate this criticizing and ranking from our own makeup, but it is very hard to do in a culture that traffics in bottom lines and top dogs.

So each time you come in second and not first, each time you are rejected and someone else is accepted, each time your literary agent fails to return your call but returns the call of a more favored writer, each time you pitch an idea which is booed but bought next year when your rival pitches it, each time your poem is smacked around or your manuscript drowned in red ink, remember: you must hold your own good opinion of yourself. The blows you receive may double you over in pain; even so, come back from the brink. Regain your good opinion of yourself. Second place, fifth place, a hundredth place, a millionth. Love yourself anyway and keep rebounding and resubmitting manuscripts.

ROLE PLAY:
Getting Criticized

Person A: You're a writer. You've just shown your friend your most recent short story, which you claim to have dashed off but which you actually labored over for the past month. You think you've done a good job; but you're still nervous about your friend's reaction. Screw up your courage and ask him/her for his/her frank opinion.

Person B: You're a friend who's just read this writer's new short story. It has many obvious flaws, it seems less strong than the work he/she was doing a year ago, and it also reminds you of a story you read recently in the *New Yorker*. You wonder aloud if your friend has read that story. You realize that since he/she has asked for your frank opinion, you have permission—even the obligation—to pick out all the flaws you can find.

Debriefing Questions

Questions for the writer to answer:

1. What was the experience like for you?
2. Do you still feel friendly toward this person?
3. Let's say that your friend had some useful things to say to you. Even so, are you inclined to show your work to friends or inclined to spare yourself the criticism?
4. How can you separate out "good" criticism from "bad" criticism? Can you articulate the filtering process?
5. When someone surprises you by not liking your writing, what will you do? What's your plan?

Questions for the writer's friend to answer:

1. What was the experience like for you?
2. Did you feel comfortable or uncomfortable criticizing your friend? Why?
3. How would you have reacted had your comments been directed at you? To what extent is it easier to criticize than to be criticized?
4. Which criticism seemed to hurt your friend the most? Which the least? Can you judge why?
5. Invent a careful "vocabulary of criticism" that is direct but not insulting. Can you come up with a few useful phrases?

Questions for the observers to answer:

1. What especially struck you about the interaction?

2. How well or poorly did the writer seem to handle the experience of being criticized by a putative friend?
3. How might the writer have handled the situation differently? Have you any suggestions?
4. How well or poorly do you handle criticism and rejection in your own life? When does it hurt or affect you the most? When the least? What makes the difference?
5. Come up with a group plan for handling criticism and rejection.

MAKING CHOICES

The first royalty statement for your new book has arrived and you discover that you have no subsidiary rights' earnings, even though your book was a book club selection and was serialized in a major magazine. What do you do?

(a) Call your literary agent and discuss the problem.
(b) Call your editor to complain and threaten an audit.
(c) Call your publisher to complain and threaten an audit.
(d) Call your local branch of the Writer's Union to lodge a complaint and get some help.
(e) Do nothing, with the hope that the earnings will show up on the next royalty statement.

The first thing to do is to take a deep breath. If you look too closely at the food in your refrigerator, you will always find mold and bacteria. If you look too closely at a royalty statement, you will always find something to make yourself sick.

But that isn't to say that a writer should tolerate being treated poorly. What is the middle way here? Discussing the matter with your literary agent is probably a good idea, especially if you see it more as an opportunity to check in with your agent and less as the first salvo in a battle with your publisher. If your agent says, "Let's wait one more royalty statement to see if the money appears," you might accept that gracefully; or you might reasonably respond by asking your agent to make a phone call to your editor to see if there's been some small oversight that can easily be corrected.

You might consider talking to your editor, or perhaps your editor's assistant, instead of your agent, especially if you like the idea of getting well-versed in all aspects of the writing life. The trick here is to ask the question calmly and give your editor plenty of time—days, certainly, but even a week or two—to look into the matter. My hunch is that someone from your publisher will call you back with some sort of answer. With luck, that answer will strike you as reasonable.

If it doesn't, then you'll have to consider what to do next. That might well be nothing. The problem is simple to state but hard to solve: at what point do you make a stink and threaten a relationship? At the very least, take several deep breaths. If you act in haste you may well repent at leisure.

Consider this an opportunity to do some personality work on yourself. Something in you probably cries out for justice and hates the idea of having your rights trampled: these are strong points in your personality. But you may also bring a myopic and unhealthy narcissism to the moment, a two-year-old's mindset, and an attitude that is demanding and unyielding, which are not strengths in your personality. You may take this as an opportunity to speak clearly and directly to someone in authority: that is a strong point in your nature. But you may take this as an opportunity to act out all the hurt you've experienced as an unrecognized and underappreciated writer: that might provide you with a split second's catharsis, but only guilt and pain afterwards.

Remember that you are bound to bring all your strengths and weaknesses, all your healthy defenses and unhealthy defenses, all your optimism and pain, to these sorts of charged interactions. So, who do you want to be? Your healthiest self? Your unhealthiest self? Look in the mirror and decide what part of your personality you want to manifest before you leap to battle.

"MIXED" NARCISSISM AND THE WRITER

The previous section leads us nicely to the subject of narcissism.

Writers are often thought of as narcissistic to the core. But narcissism is a concept saddled with all sorts of contradictions and multiple meanings. S. R. Welt and W. G. Herron explained in *Narcissism and the Therapist*, "Narcissism can be seen as pathology and as an essential part of development. It has been considered a stage of libidinal development, a sexual perversion, a type of relationship as well as a lack of relationships, and an aspect of self-esteem." G. O. Gabbard, in *Psychodynamic Psychiatry in Clinical Practice*, argued that "the term *narcissistic* is rarely used as a compliment to refer to someone with healthy self-esteem. On the contrary, the term is much more commonly used pejoratively as a synonym for 'son of a bitch,' especially when referring to colleagues and acquaintances whom we find unpleasant. Since we all struggle with narcissistic issues, we must always be wary of the potential for hypocrisy in labeling others as narcissistic."

The narcissism called unhealthy or pathological is conceptualized by psychologists as an internal state of splitting caused in the crucible of childhood, such that one part of the psyche unreasonably overvalues the worth of the self and another part of the psyche unfortunately undervalues the worth of the self. Each component affects and is affected by the other and the overall dynamic prevents the creation or integration of a "true self." The original narcissistic wounds cause the formation of a personality structure built around a pair of drives: the drive to be held as important by others, to be praised, indulged, believed, deferred to, even revered, and also the drive never to be unmasked, to never be shown up as flawed, fallible, unimportant, worthless. The first drive leads to grandiosity and the second to defensiveness.

But it is not that writers are typically either healthy narcissists *or* unhealthy narcissists. It is rather that they are both, at one and the same time. In ourselves, we see the consequences of self-inflation and self-deflation wrapped together in a single package. What writer isn't inclined to react internally to criticism with rage or shame? What writer doesn't expect to be noticed as special, even without any past or current achievements to his credit? What writer doesn't believe that his problems are unique and can only be understood by people who are special in their own right? What writer doesn't feel a basic sense of entitlement, as if he were put on earth to shine with a special light? What writer isn't regularly preoccupied with fantasies of unlimited success, brilliance, or ideal love? Which are the healthy parts and which the unhealthy parts of these beliefs and reactions?

Theorists typically argue that unhealthy narcissism is a sign of a failure of maternal empathy coupled with early experiences of loss and rejection. But the matter can hardly be that straightforward. It seems to me that we must consider the possibility that even an ideal childhood will produce a "mixed" narcissism, one with both healthy and unhealthy features, by virtue of the fact that high self-esteem comes with its own shadow side built right in.

Who is more important to me than me? Why shouldn't I consider myself first, trust myself more than I trust you, or want more things for myself than I want for you? You want me to have high self-esteem but you want there to be no negative consequences to that high self-esteem? What can you be thinking! If I am a healthy narcissist, I must have the kind of belief in myself that demands that I "arrogantly and grandly" believe that I should do exactly what I think I should do. Healthy narcissism by itself will produce many of the behaviors and attitudes that we are too quick to associate with unhealthy narcissism.

If healthy self-esteem by its very nature casts a long shadow on personality formation, producing its particular brand of arrogance, grandiosity, and relationship difficulties, and if, alongside this healthy narcissism, we also have deflation present, arising from wounding childhood experiences or from blows to self-esteem that are endemic to the creative life, then we can expect to see exactly what we do see. We can expect to see a person with real assets and real liabilities. The challenge is to sort these narcissisms out. When we look in the pool and see our reflection, we need to do a finer job of appraising what we see than young Narcissus managed.

GETTING SOME HELP

Maire Farrington is a Bay Area psychotherapist who works with writers and runs writing groups. She provided the following piece.

Walking the Path Alone Together

I met Alison just as she was emerging from the cocoon of academia, after earning a Ph.D. in education. She phoned one day, intrigued with my career path, full of curiosity about the writer's life. "How did you get where you are?" she wanted to know.

Over lattes at a local cafe, I answered her many questions about why and how I became a writer. Her undisguised admiration for my seemingly mundane accomplishments caught me completely off-guard. "You've made it," she said. "You're doing what you want to be doing." The affirming words caused me to take pause and see with new eyes how the many steps I'd taken over the years—some quite small, some nothing less than the proverbial leap of faith—had brought me to this place where, sure enough, I was "doing what I want to be doing."

> "Writing is not a profession but a vocation of unhappiness."
>
> —Georges Simenon
>
> **What are the sources of this unhappiness? Which can be ameliorated?**

I had no idea that Alison herself had recently begun taking the first tentative steps toward realizing her dream of becoming a writer. When she gingerly pulled a thin manuscript from her bag and cradled it to her chest with crossed arms, I began to understand: she was trying to find her own path. With a look of utter vulnerability Alison started to explain that she had begun writing on a subject that she hoped to develop into a nonfiction book. "I've only told a couple of people," she said. Their responses hadn't been encouraging: "Are you sure you have anything new to say?" was the gist of it. Which, of course, did nothing to alleviate Alison's own doubts. Maybe her friends were right. Who was she, after all, to think that she could write a book?

"I'm looking for a collaborator—someone to write it with me," Alison said. She proceeded to share her plans for the project, her fragility metamorphosing into a strong sense of purpose. There was no lack of enthusiasm or clarity as she outlined her ideas for the book. She spoke quite confidently about the topic, clearly a passion of hers. I questioned her motives for seeking a co-author; she obviously possessed the resources needed to write the book herself. Tears spilled down Alison's face as she revealed what she was truly searching for: "I just want someone to hold my hand through this," she said.

Several years ago, as part of my psychotherapy practice, I began facilitating support groups for women writers. Writers join these groups seeking to work through difficulties such as writer's block, procrastination, or lack of confidence in their work. Some of their questions are more easily addressed than others; many are not wholly answerable. Certain concerns lend themselves to practical advice: how to make time for writing when one depends on an unrelated job for income, how to move past a "stuck" place in a particular piece, how to solicit an agent.

More insidious are the questions that will not go away with an inventiveness of scheduling, a change in angle or approach, or a well-written query letter. Questions like: What will happen if my honesty alienates my friends or family? How can I be authentic in my writing when it means exposing this very personal side of myself? How do I know that my writing is really any good (worth anything)? When I have set aside time to write, why is it that I'd prefer to clean out the shower grout with a toothpick? What do I do when writing is pure torture, but not writing is even worse? Why am I afraid of what I want most?

As in a conventional therapy group, it is much more than the exchange of practical advice that facilitates transformation. A synergy develops when writers come together for a common purpose, not the least of which is to find relief from the isolation that is intrinsic to their work. The group becomes stronger than the individual, the sum of its parts even greater than the whole. The healing begins with acceptance, with the honoring of each other's process, with the freedom to say, "I am a writer," and not be questioned.

It continues when a writer is allowed to articulate, first to herself, then aloud to others, her discouragement, her most private fears, the irrational rantings of her merciless inner critic. It's found in the bearing witness to, and being witnessed by, others familiar with the resolute belief in oneself, the tremendous faith that is required to pursue a dream when the rewards may be few and perhaps a long time in coming. The group becomes a holding place where writers draw upon the unifying power of the whole and summon the courage to open the doors of dark dusty closets where fears reside and, armed with compassion, meet them face to face in the half-light.

Such a group offers to writers a place where nobody says, "How much money do you make?" or "When are you going to get a real job?" What is offered instead is a place where others believe in them, so that it may be easier to believe in themselves. Nodding heads and knowing eyes convey unmistakably, "I've been there. I am there. I understand." The triumphant smiles returned as one small step is taken, progress is made, an "impossible" success is celebrated, come from those who know firsthand the sheer exhilaration of accomplishing a creative goal, and what a struggle it has been to get there. Who know what it is like to have shared their dreams only to be met with cynicism, indifference, disparagement. In this community, writers may again beckon from the wings those dreams, and allow them to take center stage.

Surrounded by those who understand from the inside the challenges of the creative life, one can dare to leave the insular comfort of familiar misery, and walk the path of the unknown, one foot in front of the other.

Alison dabbed at her face with a tissue, apologizing for her tears. No need for apologies, I assured her. What she was going through was perfectly normal—there was nothing wrong with wanting someone to hold her hand. I related some of my own experiences in dealing with the less than supportive comments of others, my own battles with discouragement, doubts, and fears. Alison's eyes met mine, shining with the radiance of someone who, having risked exposure, having brought to light a previously concealed side of herself, has met with true understanding. She spoke her next words with vitality and conviction: "I believe we should recognize the bigness in ourselves, and the bigness in others. We need to affirm that bigness."

When it comes to the writer's life, there are no formulas, no easy answers, no "quick fixes." Each of us must still find our own path. But we can acknowledge the "bigness" in ourselves and hold a mirror to others when they lose sight of the bigness in themselves. We walk in solitude as we work in solitude, but we can hold each other's hands along the way.

Hit Parade of Top 60 Writers' Challenges

In this chapter and in the previous chapters I've named many challenges that writers face, and I'll be naming more in subsequent chapters. Here I'd like to stop and collect sixty writers' challenges and for each challenge point out one thing a writer might do to meet it. This is not necessarily the best thing a writer might do and it is certainly not the only thing a writer might do, but it is one thing.

This list is not exhaustive but it does look exhausting. How could any writer meet so many challenges? But if I were to make a similar list of all of life's challenges, that list would number into the hundreds of thousands of items. On it would be everything from avoiding suspect mushrooms to filling the God-sized hole in the postmodern heart. Any long list of challenges is always misleading, because we meet a lot of them as a matter of course without giving them a second thought. Do you stop the car to pick and eat mushrooms growing by the side of the road? Not unless you're trained in mushroom hunting or have a death wish. The challenge of not stopping when we see a wild mushroom is the kind of challenge we meet automatically.

I'm alphabetizing these sixty challenges and not grouping them together by topic to emphasize the fact that they interconnect and interpenetrate. A depression is in the person, but it may be about work or about the world. Envy is in the person, but it may be more about the inequities of book advances and the rise of the celebrity book than about the basic personality of the writer. So it seems better and truer to avoid making false groupings, even though that leaves us with an unlinked list.

Here we go, then.

> *"Boozing does not necessarily have to go hand in hand with being a writer, as seems to be the concept in America. I therefore solemnly declare to all young men trying to become writers that they do not actually have to become drunkards first."*
>
> —Nelson Aldrich
>
> **Are you drinking too much? What will you do?**

* *Addictions*. Honor the power of your addiction before you even think about challenging it. Say, "Wow, you are one heck of an addiction!" Drop the idea that your addiction might be easy to eradicate and surrender to the fact that it has a real hold on you.

* *Agents*. Better understand what an agent does by trying to agent a friend's work. Say to your friend, "Give me a month to try to sell your novel." Try to figure out which editors to call. See what it feels like to call them. See if you can do it. See what you learn.

* *Aging*. Some things get harder as we grow older, but many things get easier. We have so many experiences to learn from! You can write better now. You can sell better now. Why? Because of your hard-earned wisdom. Try to articulate that wisdom: what have you learned and how will you use it?

* *Alcoholism*. Start by telling yourself, "I can have a good life without alcohol." Make that your mantra. Say it so often that you come to believe it. Until a life without alcohol seems possible, it isn't.
* *Alienation*. Go to a playground and watch the children. When you write, think of the children. You're actually writing for them: for the innocent, serious part in each of us.
* *Ambition*. You don't want to extinguish the fire in your belly. But you don't want to let it incinerate you, either. Dream big but live a life so rounded and rich that setbacks only scorch you a little.
* *Anger*. Silently scream. Scream and scream. The anger is real, justified, and a killer. Scream and release it.
* *Anxiety*. Anxiety is an amazing antagonist. It lurks everywhere. Having trouble deciding whether to write this story or that one? Look for the anxiety. Fortunately, it often vanishes once spotted and named.
* *Arrogance*. There's necessary arrogance and unnecessary arrogance. Learn the difference. Your life depends on fostering the one and eradicating the other.
* *Blocks*. Reframe your block as performance anxiety. Say, "I guess I'm worried about my upcoming performance." Then perform anyway. Supply your own applause.
* *Boredom*. Existential crises end when meaning returns. List three meaningful things to do and do one of them. If you can't generate even a brief list, go out and jog. Maybe meaning is waiting for you by the side of the trail.
* *Career*. Locate an honest writer who's published a lot. Listen to her explanations. Consider them seriously. Take notes. Find a second writer. Are they saying the same things? Now you have something to go on.
* *Chaos*. Make "to do" lists on erasable boards. Pull the essentials out of the chaos. Lock onto your current writing idea and do not let go until it has grown whole and beautiful.
* *Commercialism*. Leave this culture or surrender to commercialism. Here, everything you write is a product with a target audience. Your publisher is selling. You are selling. Keep as much of your honor and dignity as you can, but recognize that here, words go to market.
* *Community*. Form a writing group whose central goal is the support of its members. If the first one doesn't work, start a second. Make some writing friends, meet at least once a month, taste a little community.

✳ *Completion*. Don't shrug away the fact that you are not completing things. Say, "I am anxious but I *will* finish." Get to the last sentence of the last page of the last revision. Then launch your piece into the marketplace.

✳ *Compromises*. Let go of the idea that an ethical person never compromises. Draw a line in the sand over which you won't cross, but don't draw it right at your feet.

✳ *Compulsions*. Get very quiet, quieter than you've ever gotten before. Whisper to your compulsion, "You are the master right now, but I am charting a course of emancipation." Then chart it.

✳ *Concentration*. Block out some time. Find a quiet place. Go there. Do some work. Stay there for hours.

✳ *Conflict*. Name the conflict out loud. "I want to write but I'm scared I'm untalented." "I want to sell this story but I'm tired of rejection." Always name the conflict; that helps it drain. Unnamed conflicts fester.

✳ *Craft*. Write a lot. A lot. Don't say that you're unable to craft beautiful things until you've given yourself years of trying. Don't say it even then! Your first piece may be grand; but what if the grand piece is destined to be your ninth, and you stop at eight? What then?

✳ *Criticism*. Build a six-foot by six-foot concrete pad in your back yard and when some criticism rocks you, go stand on your pad. Feel its solidity. Let the tremors subside and then ask yourself, "Is there something in this criticism I need to hear or should I just chuck it?"

✳ *Cynicism*. Be a cynic. But be careful. Cynicism is a greased pole on the way to nihilism. Are you sliding? Drop the cynicism and acknowledge the pain and anger underneath.

✳ *Day jobs*. It would be better not to need a day job. But you probably will. Try to find one with some built-in meaning. If you can't, think about securing a second career in addition to writing. This plan has its drawbacks, too, but it may prove more satisfactory than decades of bad day jobs.

✳ *Depression*. If you're prone to severe depressions, don't let pride stand between you and the latest anti-depressants. For some people, they are miraculously useful. Don't say, "Only hopeless failures take such things." Say instead, "I want to live and I'll do what it takes."

✳ *Discipline*. Imagine that discipline can only be coaxed, not forced. Seduce a little more discipline out of yourself. Say, "Let's just sit together by the computer, baby, you and me, and play some inner jazz. Let's improvise."

* *Editors.* Get to know one editor. Take her to lunch. Study how she thinks. Listen to what she says. Then get to know another editor. Then another. If there aren't three editors in your town, spend a week where they are: say, at a writers' conference. At a recent Romance Writers of America conference, sixty-five editors attended. Wouldn't you have learned a lot?

* *Envy.* Cry a good, hard cry. Surrender to the painful feelings. Then determine to rethink the marketplace and plot out your own path to success. Or just feel successful.

* *Fame.* If you're famous and hating it, imagine trying to publish as an unknown. Is that what you want? If it is, do it. If it isn't, modulate your groaning. If you're not famous and craving it, transform that desire into concrete action. Sit still and use your billions of brain cells to answer the question, "If I must be famous, what's my plan?"

> "Writers seldom wish other writers well."
>
> —Saul Bellow
>
> **What can you do with your feelings of envy?**

* *Guilt.* Yes, you haven't written enough, or well enough, or published enough, or published at all. But release all that guilt. Roll that ten-ton boulder off your chest. To prevent it from rolling back, write more, write better, and work harder at selling.

* *Imagination.* If you fear you aren't imaginative enough, just imagine. Dream up a world. Create a setting. Conjure a plot. Make myth. Invent Wonderland. Sit down, shut your eyes, and imagine.

* *Insecurity.* You may never gain financial security. You may never feel secure that the book you're writing will turn out well. But there are other securities available to you. There is the security of an intimate relationship—that is, if both partners are trustworthy and willing to love. Try your hand at that kind of security.

* *Intimacy.* Do not look for love; look for ways to love. Act from the heart, be kinder and more considerate, but also expect and demand some reciprocity.

* *Isolation.* Go to your local coffee house and talk to the first person you see. Say, "How are you today?" After awhile, excuse yourself and move on to another table. Spend the day with members of your species.

✳ *Language.* Writing is a love affair with language. Write crisp sentences. Write flowery sentences. Write things that make no sense and then improve them. Write simple things and then add subtlety. Write complex things and then simplify. Get a Ph.D. in your own language.

✳ *Loneliness.* Are you erecting walls around yourself? Get a sledgehammer and knock them down. Step out of the rubble. Go find a likely stranger and put out your hand.

> *"Writing is for the most part a lonely and unsatisfying occupation. One is tied to a table, a chair, a stack of paper."*
>
> —Graham Greene
>
> **Name twelve cures for the loneliness of the long-distance writer.**

✳ *Love.* Love the person in the mirror. Love your current book. Love the decent people who come your way. Find some way to love the world as it is.

✳ *Mania.* You will have to judge whether your mania is enthusiasm and energy all mixed together or a clinical mania heralding the onset of a severe depression. There are good manias and bad manias: clinical mania cries out for psychotherapy and psychopharmacology.

✳ *Marketplace.* Go to the nearest big book fair. In my neck of the woods, the San Francisco Book Fair happens every November. Stop at each of the scores of booths. Who's selling what? What's being sold? Talk to the reps. Study their wares. Say, "This is a charming book! How many copies of it are you hoping to sell?" Start to piece together the marketplace puzzle.

✳ *Narcissism.* You are the beauty in life. Enjoy a healthy narcissism. You are also the ugliness in life. Curtail your unhealthy narcissism. Live by the motto, "First, do no harm." Before you criticize or kill with a stare, ask yourself, "Is hurting my best policy here?"

✳ *Obscurity.* You may write and never get recognized. To say that obscurity is the common lot of writers is not to reduce its sting. Obscurity hurts like hell. Is it time to try to write something that millions of people want to read? Is it time to make another effort at becoming the exception? Or are grieving and acceptance the necessary answers?

✳ *Organization.* Use erasable boards, computer technology, logs, notebooks, anything and everything to help you do a better job of managing your ideas, submissions, and business efforts. There is too much to keep in one's head. Argue yourself into the habit of organization.

✳ *Products.* Your products will start to accumulate around the house. Try not to let them make you anxious or angry. Give each one its own place. Give each one a little time each month, as you sit with it and decide if it's in showing shape and, if it is, where you mean to send it.

✳ *Publishing.* For one day, be a publisher. You have two thousand back-listed titles to sell. You have a hundred new titles slated to be published this year. You know that only ten of them will be really successful. What criteria would you use to buy your next manuscript?

✳ *Readers.* Get one reader—maybe a buddy. Get a second reader—maybe an agent. Go after one reader at a time. If they tell you something, listen. When you can't count the readers of your work on the fingers of your hands, congratulations!

✳ *Rejection.* Rejection only means that someone didn't want the work. Bad things are rejected and good things are rejected. Stupid things are rejected and smart things are rejected. You can't tell anything about the work from the fact that it's been rejected. Look at the work again: if you still like it, try just that much harder to sell it.

✳ *Relationships.* Reframe relationships as gains of connectedness rather than as losses of freedom. Write to an author in your genre and say, "Give me two pieces of advice." Enclose a stamped, self-addressed envelope. Write to the editor acknowledged in the book you're reading and say, "What do you look for in an author?" Yes, she probably won't answer. But risk relating anyway.

✳ *Self-censorship.* Let the truth out. You'll feel less embarrassed and less ashamed than you fear. Enrich your writing with the truth: speaking the truth ennobles you and helps your readers heal and grow.

✳ *Self-deception.* Print these words of Anatole France's in big, blue letters on cardboard and mount them over your mantel: "It is in the ability to deceive oneself that the greatest talent is shown." Is there a particular truth you need to admit? Go ahead and admit it.

✳ *Self-destruction.* Stop the hashish. Stop the fifths of vodka in the freezer. Stop the self-hatred. Stop the carelessness, which loses friends and makes enemies. Stop! Build rather than destroy.

✳ *Solitude.* Problems of all sorts prevent us from obtaining the blessings of solitude. If solitude is eluding you, find an empty room right now, put on your molded ear plugs, and do not leave the room for two or three hours. Launch into some fantastic writing.

✳ *Space.* Who invades your space? Just say, "I'll be available after lunch," and shut the door. If you don't mean it, don't say it; if they won't listen, ask yourself, "Why won't they allow me a few hours of quiet?" Is quiet not permitted in your house? Gather the family together and have a discussion about the sanctity of silence.

✳ *Stamina.* Good writing and successful publishing may be more victories of stamina than anything else. Get physically fit. Get emotionally fit. What if it takes years to write beautifully or to sell anything? Get and stay as fit as possible.

✳ *Suffering.* When you grieve about your failed writing, your lack of success, or your disarrayed life, the pain is all too real. It sears and burns. If there is any antidote, it must be happiness. Can you add even a little happiness to your life? Please think that you can.

✳ *Suicidal feelings.* Do not keep a gun around the house. Do not stockpile pills. Do not pick out a favorite spot on the bridge from which to jump. When your suicidal thoughts coalesce into a plan, cry out, "No! This isn't what I want!" Speak about your pain, even just to a friendly stranger on the other end of a suicide hot line.

✳ *Survival.* Survival requires luck. Make your own. Write lots; write well; meet marketplace players; learn the game. Nothing beats luck!—your survival depends on making some for yourself.

✳ *Time.* When we pay no attention to our writing, time speeds by and years slip away. But in the time it takes to watch a bad movie we could write eight pages of our book. So years are too short, if we aren't writing; but hours are very long, if we are.

✳ *Unfairness.* An evolutionary biologist chuckles at the word "unfair" as it applies to individuals and species. But if he lost his family in a car wreck he'd take that personally and maybe even die of a broken heart. If you never have a bestseller, there will be tears to shed. So shed them; and, if you're able, still keep writing.

✳ *Work.* Writing is real work. Let go of the hope that writing can be easy or that selling can be easy. Let go of the hope that you can avoid criticism and rejection. You may have some easy writing and selling days, but don't count on them.

✳ *World.* The world is as it is. The world wants what it wants. Fight the world: that's the ethical path. Don't fight the world: that's the path to success. Fight and don't fight the world simultaneously. Imagine that there's an answer to this riddle and that you're the one to find it.

INTENDING TO CONTINUE

There are a lot of challenges. But their timing can also be challenging. It's one thing to feel untalented away from the computer but talented as soon as you sit down to write. That wouldn't be so bad. But the opposite is a direr problem. Many of the challenges we face as writers hit us while we're writing. So a special preparedness is required: we need to be prepared *while we write* for the arrival of demons and earthquakes.

Generally we prepare for something and then we do it. We get ready, we rehearse, we clear our mind, we do whatever it takes so that our intentions and our actions come together. We get ready and then we act. Think of the way an actor prepares before he or she goes on stage. Laurence Olivier expressed it this way: "We must never shirk the preparation in the wings, the practicing of the old self-hypnotic act to transform ourselves completely before we step onto the stage."

Even if we don't do this kind of preparing as often as we would like, we find the concept easy to understand. Prepare, then do. But what is even more important is preparing *while doing*. The fielder not only fields the ball—he also prepares to throw it. If he only "did the fielding," he would not be in a position to throw. The writer writes but also intends to keep on writing. If she didn't intend to keep at her writing, every little doubt or mistake would stop her. *She writes, but she also prepares herself to keep writing.*

Are you prepared to keep writing when you sit down to write? Or are you only prepared to become sad and discouraged? Are you prepared to weather the inevitable writing storms that arise? Or are you primed to give up and call yourself a fool and a no-talent idiot? Are you prepared to move on to the next paragraph, the next page, the next thousand words, the next section, no matter what? Or are you ready to leap up and cry, "Thank God, I managed twelve words!" Get prepared. One challenge is starting; but another is continuing.

FOOD FOR THOUGHT

"It is better to have a permanent income than to be fascinating."—Oscar Wilde
Where will the money come from while you write? What can be done about the fact that earning a living is draining and time-consuming?

"Unbearable solitude—I cannot believe it or resign myself to it."—Albert Camus
To what extent is your solitude unbearable? Can you bear it anyway or lessen its unbearability?

"Part of my disease is anger."—*Jim Cody*
Since it is hard to write and even harder to fashion a career
as a writer, many writers grow angry and resentful. Have you?

"After ecstasy, the laundry."—*Zen saying*
What about the ordinary and the everyday? How well do you handle them?

*"I believe the saddest news one has to give any young
writer just setting out is that very few good writers are
able to support themselves by their writing."*—*Peter Taylor*
You may have to work at unsatisfying day jobs, start a second career,
live in poverty, or be supported by others. What about all that?

*"Recognition is everything you write for; it's much more
than the money. You want your books to be valued.
It's a basic aspiration of the serious writer.*—*William Kennedy*
How long can you go without some recognition?
How long can you toil away in obscurity?

*"Poets are like baseball pitchers. They have their moments.
The intervals are the tough things."*—*Robert Frost*
How satisfactory is the life you lead between creative efforts?
Are there some improvements to be made?

*"Most writers are in a state of gloom a good deal of the time;
they need perpetual reassurance."*—*John Hall Wheelock*
Who or what reassures you?

*"If a writer's ego ever wilts, he is ruined. Every morning he has
to persuade himself, all over again, that putting words on paper
is the most important thing in the world."*—*John Fischer*
Are you persuaded that writing is the most important thing
in the world? Is this an illusion worth maintaining?

*"Art! What a concept! It saved my life! A place
where you can do as you please!"*—*William Wiley*
But what about those places where you can't exert any control? What about them?

"If I feel physically as if the top of my head were
taken off, I know that is poetry."—Emily Dickinson
How do you survive the effort of writing? What are your methods?

"Critics desire our blood, not our pain."—Friedrich Nietzsche
You will have your critics. What will you do?

"As a fiction writer I find it convenient not to believe things.
Not to disbelieve them either, just move them into a realm
where everything is held in suspension."—William Gass
How can you live holding everything in suspension?

"It is never too late to be who you might have been."—George Eliot
Is it too late? If not, what will you do?

"To write well, to write passionately, to be less inhibited,
to be warmer, to be more self-critical, to recognize the power
of as well as the force of lust, to write, to love."—John Cheever
There's a lot to do. Will you manage?

6 A Writer's Strengths

A writer is a person who says, "I will use myself in order to know for myself." The presence or absence of this particular outlook and self-relationship determines how a person will spend her time, employ her mind, and view the world.

When she asserts that she means to think her own thoughts and learn about the universe in her own way, she enters into a self-relationship with far-reaching consequences. To the world she may look idiosyncratic, because she is carving out her own trail; arrogant, grandiose, or self-centered, because she is putting a fundamental premium on her own ideas and her own conception of the universe; introverted, because in order to have her thoughts she must think them, and to think them she will need to daydream, calculate, and engage in other mental processes; and skeptical, because she necessarily doubts the meanings and methods of others. We see an outline of the "creative personality" emerging as a function of the self-relationship a person enters into when she says, "I will know for myself and be exactly myself."

The goals of such a person are radically different from the goals of most people. The goals of the writer are not primarily to conform, to fit in, to be liked, to make money, or even to survive. Some findings from the psychological literature on creative adolescents help us better understand this self-relationship. The researchers J.W. Getzels and M. Csikszentmihalyi, in their study of 200 full-time art students, found that their subjects scored a full standard deviation or more below the norm on the Scale of Economic and Social Value. That is, these art students deviated significantly from the common money-making and meaning-making values held by their society. Getzels and a second researcher, P.W. Jackson, in a comparative study of "highly intelligent" versus "highly creative" adolescents, concluded:

> The creative adolescent seemed to possess the ability to free himself from the usual, to "diverge" from the customary. He seemed to enjoy the risk and uncertainty of the unknown. In contrast, the high-I.Q. adolescent seemed to possess to a high degree the ability and the need to focus on the usual, to be "channeled and controlled" in the direction of the right answer—the customary. He appeared to shy away from the risk and the uncertainty of the unknown and to seek out the safety and security of the known.

For the writer, there is no knowledge except personal knowledge and no meaning without it. A writer "knows nothing" about the two girls she feels compelled to send down the river on an adventure until she sends them there in imagination and transcribes the adventure. The average person falsely believes that he or she "already knows," "shouldn't know," "can never know," or "needs the right answer." The writer has a very different outlook. She needs to really know. This is a writer's primary strength and distinguishes her from the ordinary person.

GROWING STRONG THROUGH FAILURE

Writers are ambitious. They want to build great new worlds and to make this old, flawed world a better place for the children. Truth, beauty, and goodness are their watchwords, as are magic, passion, logic, intuition, knowledge, and humanity. Out of these building-blocks they attempt to forge their spirited creative works. But the writer's painful secret, which may be God's secret as well, is that failure comes more often than success does. It is not so easy to build new worlds. It is the opposite of easy.

> *"Try again. Fail again. Fail better."*
>
> —Samuel Beckett
>
> **Is learning from your experiences one of your strengths?**

Writers with real accomplishments to their credit will be happy to tell you about all the books that didn't work, which may amount to half or two-thirds of their efforts. There were the books where a hundred pages got done but the book had to be abandoned because it had no life to it. There were the books that got entirely written but that turned out seriously flawed, because the writer wasn't ready or because the flaw just naturally appeared, as a flaw in pottery can appear in the firing process. Writers could tell you all about these things but we hate to hear these stories, because it depresses and frightens us that so much failure is both possible and actually happens.

But there is no creativity without failure. Failure may even be at the heart of creativity, just as misfits and mutants have their honored place in the process of evolution. Honoring the writing process means stumbling but getting up, writing whole miserable books, throwing out ideas and beautiful lines that do not fit, nursing depressions and surviving depressions, living through good manias and bad manias, getting one's work insulted (today I received an edited manuscript whose margins were peppered with "lame!"s and "flabby!"s), and a thousand other things which are inevitable parts of the process. It means accepting all of this and influencing for the better that which can be influenced.

Dishonoring the process means wanting it all to be otherwise and acting as if it could be otherwise. It means not showing your work when it is ready because you fear its reception. It means researching instead of thinking or making things up instead of researching. It means being a drunk all weekend. It means not being arrogant enough to write and being too arrogant to listen to others. It means not doing what one knows one should do and doing what one knows one shouldn't do. Above all, it means refusing to accept the place of failure in the creative process and the creative life. Mere mortals may want to avoid failure, but gods and writers accept that failure is their lot all too frequently.

Writers can accept this intellectually. But their actual failures hurt. After a well-received concert of Handel's music, the King exclaimed to the famous composer, "The audience was very greatly entertained!" A downcast Handel replied, "Did I only entertain them? I had hoped to make them better!" What sort of odd reaction is this? It's the reaction of a creator with the loftiest ideals feeling as if he'd failed, even though the audience was shouting its approval. When even successes can feel like failures, what a strain that puts on all creators!

I believe that letting this secret out of the bag and actively thinking about all of this—the nature of the creative process, the naturalness of failure, the way that part-successes often do not feel good enough—helps us survive. But it is hard to think about. I remember chatting in an airport restaurant with the publisher of several of my books, Jeremy Tarcher, about a book I was considering writing. I had done a pair of books called *Fearless Creating* and *Fearless Presenting* and was thinking about doing a third in the "series," to be called *Fearless Thinking*. We concluded that such a book would be too hard to sell. Too few people would be willing to suffer the uncomfortable feelings that come with trying to think.

But if we do not think about the place of failure in the creative process, then when we write a miserable first novel we'll chastise ourselves, retreat from future efforts, and shut our creativity off. If we do not understand that failure, mistakes, missteps, wrong turns, bad ideas, shoddy workmanship, half-baked theories, and other sad events are part of the process, if we romanticize the process and make believe that creativity comes with a happy face attached, then when we encounter our own rotten work we will be forced to conclude that we do not have what it takes. We do have what it takes. What it takes is learning and recovering from our own mistakes.

I teach a class each semester at St. Mary's College called "Personal and Professional Assessment." It is a class for middle-aged adults who are returning to school to get their bachelor's degrees after a long absence from the classroom. Their primary task in my class is to write five "experiential learning essays" on five subjects of their own choosing. These managers, policewomen, firefighters, winemakers, and salespeople have written very little for years and strongly doubt that they have the skills they need to do the required writing. I start right in and teach them essay basics—how to analyze, synthesize, and evaluate, how logical arguments are built—but I also let them know that their first efforts may look wretched. I ask them to succeed but I give them real permission to fail.

I encourage them to think about the subjects they've chosen to write about—to grow quiet and to begin writing—and to ignore the horribleness of their first drafts. Slowly but surely they manage to do this. They begin to think about a subject like divorce or child abuse in a deep way; they stop thinking about the skills they lack. They begin to quiet their inner demons. They start to feel less frightened as their computers boot up and less intimidated by the blank screen when it appears. They continue to feel a little anxious, but they learn that such anxiety is normal. And maybe it isn't even anxiety. Maybe it's just excitement! Whatever those butterflies mean, they really don't matter.

These engaged student writers go deep and write well. They focus on the subject at hand and not on themselves or their frailties. They start to say things like, "All right, I've bitten off a big thing here. But no problem!" Rather than doubt themselves, they focus on their ideas. Despite these improvements, they still sometimes write not-very-good essays. But often they write quite well. Some of the things they write are as good as the pieces you see in journals and magazines. This is remarkable and a sign that almost anyone can do the writing he or she dreams of doing, if only the inevitable failures that arise can be normalized, embraced, and forgiven.

Books do not go unwritten because the writer has trouble remembering whether to use "its" or "it's." They do not go unwritten because the writer has trouble deciding whether, in the world she is creating, she will have her rose bushes flower in winter or lie dormant. They do not go unwritten because the writer can't write sentences (we all can), because the writer can't write paragraphs (we all can), or because the writer can't write chapters (we all can, with practice). Books go unwritten because the writer is afraid of failing. She is afraid of disappointing herself, wasting her time, and looking like an idiot. The specter of failure kills her chances for success.

We agree with Handel, that creators have profound work to do. We set our sights high. We want to express the mystery of reality in such a way that human beings become better. We want to make worlds, to explain this world, to catch magic as it flies past, and to become living magic. We are not conceited in holding these views, we are simply identifying and affirming our role in the culture. What is that role? To guard the good and to make things better. But to create and to become a role model we need to think about failure more than we do. We need to think about its reality, its naturalness, even its ubiquity. Failure is a painful subject, but to keep secret about it is worse.

If each success requires ten failures, then count each failure as a blessing on the road to success. For our successes to mount, so must our failures.

MAKING CHOICES

A small scandal has erupted locally, followed by a news frenzy. One of your local telegenic religious leaders is being interviewed everywhere about what constitutes proper values and about what God wants. Do you:

(a) Pull the plug on your TV?
(b) Scream back at the TV whenever he comes on?
(c) Smile your best ironic smile and go about your business?
(d) Write a scathing letter-to-the-editor about know-nothing religious leaders?
(e) Decide to write a smart, useful book disputing the authority of religious leaders and the existence of a God with a beard?

The average person who happens to feel strongly about something is remarkably restricted in his or her range of responses. People tend to be able only to swallow their thoughts and feelings, turning them into stress and even illness, or displace them by getting angry at the dog or the clerk at the market, or air them but in no better way than by throwing a shoe at the TV. Some may go as far as writing a letter-to-the-editor, feeling the satisfaction of articulating their thoughts and venting their spleen in several carefully crafted paragraphs. But the writer has another option. He or she can decide to fight back with whole books.

A writer can decide to fight back against the death camps or the torture of political prisoners with words. A writer can decide

> *"I shall not weary of testifying. I consider myself responsible, not to society, which dictates fashion and taste suited to its environment and its period, but to youth, to the coming generations, which are left stranded in a blitzed world."*
>
> —Oskar Kokoschka
>
> **Have you the strength to testify?**

to fight back against nuclear proliferation with words. A writer can decide to fight back against insufficient funding for breast cancer research with words. A writer can decide to fight back against abuses, tyrannies, high crimes, and misdemeanors with words. A writer can decide to fight back against any untruth or half-truth he or she encounters. A writer can even decide to fight back against the universe itself by writing angrily and existentially.

Words count. Words matter. In many places, real bravery is shown by the men and women who put out the anti-government newspapers and the anti-gangster leaflets and pamphlets, who dispute the powerful and point a finger at everyday evil, and this bravery can and does make positive things happen. That this change is not long-lasting is a testament to the dark underbelly of human nature, but these brave writers are still the human race's best hope—the best hope for the exploited child worker, the ritually abused young girl, the threatened democracy, the arrested dissident.

For all of a writer's weaknesses, for all of the ways in which a writer is challenged, this is still his or her supreme strength: to be able to point a finger. It takes no great feat of strength to point a finger, only great courage. For that finger may well get chopped off. But when a writer stands up and pens the words "I accuse . . . ," the whole world trembles. Governments prepare to topple. Scoundrels run for cover. The small voice of truth clears its throat and the whole world stops and prepares to listen.

A WRITER'S PERSISTENCE

How many people would continue toiling away at their work if they were not paid? Some would—but most would not. If the work is boring and just keeps the wheels of the world mechanically spinning, if the work only lines somebody else's pockets and does no good, if the work is unchallenging and makes no use of one's innate capacities, then there better be a paycheck at the end of the month. But writers are lucky, not that writing earns so many of them so little money, but that the work itself makes use of their hearts and minds.

This is a central "writer's strength": that the work he or she has chosen to do is worth doing. The following piece was provided by Roccie Austin Hill, executive director of the Bay Area environmental nonprofit organization Earthshare and a lifelong writer.

Two Important Things I Know About Success
Of the thousands and thousands of us who are writers in this country, few have the luxury of doing it for a living. We work as teachers or lawyers or

Website designers: we work at anything that will buy us that precious time, dazed and alone in front of a computer screen, waiting for that perfect, magic combination of words.

My own life has been just this: accidentally building a career while stealing those "spare time" writing moments. I have worked in more-than-full-time jobs for over twenty years, and yet have always considered the paying job as the marginal thing, the enemy thing which usurps my real job of writing. Maintaining a writer's desire and rhythm against a backdrop of day jobs and families and bills and birthdays was a struggle for me until I discovered two important things.

Twenty-five years ago I was in college in southern California, in some hot, bright, hopeful beach community, among students who believed like all of us, that they could have anything if only they worked hard enough. It was there that a writing teacher laid the fatal curse by telling me, "One day you will be a rich and successful writer, but never lose the ability just to lie in a field someplace and have fun writing." In this one sentence he put together the truest thing and the dumbest thing I have ever heard about writing, and it has taken me years to figure out which is which.

> "Whatever becomes of the work, the occupation of writing has been a real boon to me. It took me out of dark and desolate reality into an unreal but happier region."
>
> —Charlotte Bronte

Isn't living vicariously in a world you create a great boon and pleasure?

Certainly, he was attempting to be encouraging, complimentary, and deep. However, I have spent my life believing that writing success was inextricably tied to money, lots of it, and that I had not measured up. I have never been successful against the standards we were using in those warm, rich southern California days: my teacher lived at Malibu in a glass-walled, television-funded pad on the beach. What I learned was his image of success, and it has taken me years to deconstruct that wealthy, white-walled, blue sea picture of a writer's good life.

We adopt our own definitions of success, often early in life. I did, and the goals and indicators had to do with novels published and the size of bank accounts. We seldom revisit these early images, and often live realities which are no longer relevant to childhood standards. Early images of success can become secret ghosts of failure if we do not regularly re-examine them. It is not that we do not succeed, but that we are careless about our goals.

I have worked in the nonprofit industry for over twenty years, and have for several years run a multimillion-dollar organization. Yet because of my early success imaging, I never considered this career achievement to be remotely connected with success. My dear writing teacher told me that success was bestsellers, and unplugging this crossed wire has been an arduous task.

So, the first thing I know about success is that it is utterly subjective, and that you may and must choose your own definition, re-examine it often, and ensure that you are struggling to live up to something which is truly relevant to you. A writer takes care with words, our identities are tied up in the way we use words, and yet most of us automatically retain parental images or media ideas for this word "success," instead of scrupulously defining it for ourselves.

Once I had managed to unplug the concept of success from the old, rarely relevant definition, I found myself floundering for a new one. I would never be able to link it to my "day job," even though my day job envelops my life and is often my night job and my weekend job—even though, for example, in my day job I am about to effect one of the largest nonprofit mergers in history, one which is truly cutting edge strategy. My identity is still, so simply, that of a writer. All the rest is only a byproduct of financial necessity. I realized that it was futile to try and think of my career accomplishments as my successes. Of course, I tell myself, they are important and I am proud, in the same way I am proud of a good tennis game or a pretty vacation photograph: but none of these is core, none defines who I am.

Ultimately, I returned to the words of that same college teacher, and the wisdom he was trying to glue to me. As with many people, he was very wrong and very right, almost simultaneously, in what he said. Only years later in my awkward struggle to define a new kind of success for myself, I realized what he was saying: ". . . never lose the ability just to lie in a field someplace and have fun writing."

The second thing I know about success is it has to do with how much you love what you do. At the time I remember thinking, "What is he talking about? Writing hurts. Writing is hard. It's never fun." In those days it was merely something I did, not something I desired to do for pleasure. I did not experience any joy in writing; putting words together took time and sweat and seldom went well until I had reached a certain threshold of pain.

Years later I finally understood that taking pleasure in doing it, in the process of writing, is what really defines success for me. It is the matches and choices and small moments of total bewilderment when words combine like magic. It is the simple pleasure and enigma of it. Feeling this is success. Success is being able to focus, to protect the process, guarding it against jobs

*and children and office memos and dry cleaning pick-ups and all the pieces
that compose a picture of normal life-stress, knowing that this vigil results in
the beguiling, confusing experience of raw joy at being within the
indomitable creative process.*

Success, it's the writing, stupid.

Q & A

How do you make a living from writing?

Most writers don't. According to Author's Guild statistics, five percent of writers who earn money by writing make a living by their writing. The rest have to do other things or get support from elsewhere. But let's be even clearer. Among those people who are earning a living by writing, most are making a living by writing for other people. They are writing speeches, technical manuals, news reports, corporate biographies, annual reports, advertising copy, and so on. Is this "making a living by writing"? You'll have to decide. But I don't think it's what most of us mean. What I think "making a living by writing" means to most of us is making a living doing the writing we want to do. Few writers get to do that.

If you want to earn a living by doing your own writing and become the exception to the rule, that one-in-a-thousand writer who gets to sit home and write books and have advances and royalty payments pay the bills, you have a lot to learn about the marketplace. But you also have a lot to learn about yourself. You will have to make use of your strengths and your wisdom, for it will be on your shoulders to turn out strong query letters, strong synopses, strong articles, strong books—to be strong in your writing, your thinking, your presentation, and your marketing. It will be on your shoulders to either learn what editors and readers want and deliver it or else produce what isn't wanted and then make your own luck in finding an audience.

The dream can come true at any time, but it will only come true for a very few. There will always be luck involved, more luck than we care to imagine; and who you number among your acquaintances, who you excite about your work, and how marketable you look can be as important or more important than how well you write. But the more you operate from strength, producing strong books and strong proposals, making bold phone calls and sending smart query letters to the appropriate people, and doing whatever else is in your power to do to be the best writer and the best salesperson you can be, the better your chances of earning a living from writing will be.

WRITING AFTER FIFTY

Worries, distractions, responsibilities, self-doubts, survival needs, and a long list of other obstacles keep people from writing. Years and then decades slip by. But as Colette wrote: "At sixty-three years of age, less a quarter, one still has plans." A writer's luck is that she can still begin to write even after many years of not-writing. Maybe at the age of fifty, sixty, or even seventy the would-be writer can still let out a sigh and whisper, "Now I'm ready."

But because the wait has been so long, enormous doubts linger. Am I too late? How much do I have to learn? Can I survive the mistakes I'm bound to make? Can I stand to be a novice? Do I have it in me to do work that's beautiful and good? Can I really begin now, after having waited so long?

As a creativity consultant, I see writers and would-be writers of every age and description. My clients who are over fifty have extra challenges to overcome but they also have extra skills to employ. Contrary to the old saw about old dogs and new tricks, they learn faster and see more clearly how to get from A to B than do young folk. They listen better; they've learned the value of listening. They balk less at entertaining advice; they're less self-conscious

> *"The history of literature is nothing but the performance by authors of feats which the best experience had declared could not be performed."*
>
> —Arnold Bennett
>
> **Are you ready to perform feats that even you didn't dream were possible?**

and ego-driven; their courage has been tested and tempered in a million encounters with life. Because they possess these "elder skills" we can work together quickly and effectively in pursuit of their long-deferred goal, to write.

The first step is always the same: to talk about dreams deferred, about old pains and mishaps, but also to notice how present these dreams remain. The next step is to make a quiet bargain: that what is in the heart will be let out finally, that this adult man or woman will sweat a little to give life to his or her dream. The third step is to touch on the matter of marketplace, to calmly but directly remind ourselves that creations in closets do not serve their purposes. The fourth step is to whisper "Ready, set, go!": to alert the brain's billions of neurons to the fact that something is really starting *right now*.

Let's take a peek at the challenges three would-be writers face and the strengths they bring to their late-in-life writing adventures.

Judith is a sixty-two-year-old mother of three grown children, recently widowed and with enough income that she doesn't have to work. She loved music as a young adult, had a natural gift for the piano, pursued liberal causes as an older adult, and has done many creative things as an "amateur," a word she reveres. But she also has the strong sense that she's failed herself, not made use of her talents, not lived up to her own expectations. She has become actively involved in a religious renewal movement, has even taught a few classes for adults and written an article or two on the subject, and what she would love to do is tackle a whole book that describes how this old religion fits into our modern times. But the thought of writing a book thoroughly daunts her.

Judith's first step is to be patient, and not only patient but really generous with her patience. She's never looked to the world like a rushed or impulsive woman and yet she's been exactly that all along, rushed and impulsive inside, fleeing especially from the possibility that she might make some mistakes. Her first step is to enter into a brand-new relationship with patience and say to herself, "I am not in a rush. I'll make my mistakes, correct them, and stay put. I'm not about to run away or hide behind the label of 'amateur.'" Her shorter mantra might be, "I am going to do this."

Harry is a highly intelligent fifty-eight-year-old whose rebellious streak and anxieties caused him to work for thirty years at a job that, while responsible and serious, never made use of his intellectual and creative abilities. Smarter and more knowledgeable than his bosses and colleagues, he's a classical music buff, a film buff, well-read in psychology, philosophy, and other esoteric subjects, and full of ideas. He has always wanted to write a screenplay and he's even had two or three screenplay ideas in mind, but beyond making a few notes he's never been able to proceed. He understands that he is restricted and even a little paralyzed by his own anxieties, but he's never formulated the basic equation that "anxiety = blockage."

Harry's first step is an extraordinarily basic one: to honor the fact that he has permission to create, even though creating, like a lot of other things, makes him anxious. That he has this basic permission ought to go without saying, and yet the barrier that stands between Harry and his screenplay is exactly this elemental. He is like someone who knows how egg whites should be folded, the temperature nuances of his oven, and the characteristics of cake yeast versus granulated yeast, but who still eats out because he doesn't know how to cook. He knows everything about cooking except how to cook, which knowledge he would gain rapidly, given all that he already knows, if only he could say to himself, "I think I'll make an omelette."

What he would then discover is that dishes can burn, dry out, or acquire an off taste, but also that dishes can turn out delicious. He would learn about actual dishes and not just about the properties of ingredients. He would make connections that can't be made in any other way except by preparing real food that is meant to be eaten. Anxiety is the culprit in all of this, and what Harry might substitute for his usual thoughts is the following one: "I am very anxious but I will write anyway." He might want to learn an anxiety management skill or two before beginning, but once he learned them he would need to just begin.

Esther is a successful magazine editor who, at sixty-five, feels just about as young as she's ever felt. Over the years she's written an article or two but her creativity has primarily manifested itself in overseeing the magazine. But for the longest time she's wanted to write a historical novel set in sixteenth-century Seville. The setting is well known to her from many trips and much reading, and the characters and plot are also pretty clear in her mind. What's wanted is the writing, which she never quite manages to do.

Esther's first step is to "retire" without retiring and to make a real commitment to the novel. She needs to reduce her activities and commitments, including, and maybe even especially, some of the entirely worthy ones. Her exercise regimen, her early morning yoga, her late evening journaling, her bread baking, her committee work for dancers with AIDS, and her editorial responsibilities, which never let up, not only take time: they occupy mind space in such a way that her book has no place to grow. As things stand, her book is crowded right out of her mind.

But which of these rich, worthy things is she to stop? One answer is that she just start each day on her novel and then continue on with her full range of activities, noticing which "fall off the plate" because she's run out of time. These she may have to mourn; or perhaps she can find a way to attend to them more irregularly, now and then rather than daily or weekly. But in any event, Esther's challenge is to "prioritize" in such a way that her novel comes first, not last. Since she has strong emotional health, directness, a good ear for language, a fine mind, and other strengths, it may be that just this single change, moving the novel up her list of priorities, will make all the difference in the world.

It turns out that people at fifty, sixty, seventy, and beyond are both sages and babes-in-the-woods. Again and again, they are surprised by what they know and by what they don't know. But what they do know for sure is that "soul" or "spirit" and "creativity" are virtual synonyms. The complete life, the healthy life, must also be a creative life, full of ideas, poetry, color, and music, full of truth, beauty, and goodness. Who knows, we may yet turn the gift of a longer life span into a renaissance, as people of great age work away in their studies, hammering out and then sharing with the world some wild, wise, and surprising things.

ROLE PLAY:
Gestalt Chair Work

You will be playing both persons A and B this role play, moving from chair A to chair B as the role play dictates.

As the person in chair A, choose a problem you are having. It could be a problem with a book you're writing, with a person you know, with yourself, with the world. Choose one that has two sides to it: a book that could go in this direction or that direction, a relationship you could stay in or leave, anger that you want to release about not being published but that you don't want to release in a damaging way. As you sit in chair A, "be" one side, and when you switch to the other chair, "be" the other side. Try having the two positions enter into a real dialogue, each telling its truth as best it can.

When you sit in chair B, really adopt position B. When you return to your original position, really adopt position A. Use your strengths to make the role play work: your ability to tolerate ambiguity, your keen imagination, your truth-telling ability, your empathic powers. Continue the role play until you've learned something you didn't know before. You might even keep going until you resolve the problem in favor of one or the other position or in favor of a solution that synthesizes both.

Debriefing Questions

Questions for the writer in position A to answer:

1. What was the experience like for you?
2. Which side of the dispute did you choose as side A? Why?
3. How did it feel to leave chair A the first time? How did it feel to leave it subsequent times?
4. If you came to some sort of resolution, how did that resolution feel?
5. If you didn't come to any resolution, what seemed to prevent that from happening?

Questions for the writer in position B to answer:

1. What was the experience like for you in the second chair?
2. Was the second position clear to you from the beginning? Did it become clearer? Did it become murkier?
3. What shifts occurred inside you as the role play progressed?
4. Would you say that this is an exercise that more uses your intellect or that more accesses your emotions?
5. How did this method of inner conflict resolution feel to you? Could you see using it in the future?

Questions for the observers to answer:

1. What especially struck you about the interaction?
2. To what extent did the writer seem to be able to really inhabit both positions?
3. What seemed to be the strengths of this sort of "gestalt chair work"? What seemed to be its weaknesses or drawbacks?
4. Does this seem like an effective way for a person to get to know and even resolve his/her problems?
5. What current writing problem or life problem would you bring to these two chairs?

AN INNER WRITER VISITS

In the following piece Susanne West, assistant professor of psychology at John F. Kennedy University, faculty member of the Psychosynthesis Training Program, and co-founder of Word Works, takes a look at the idea of the "inner writer" and the writer's strengths of self-communication and self-understanding.

Inside One Writer's Mind

Zoe Songbird presented herself to me upon my invitation seven years ago, at a point where I was particularly stuck in my writing. My poems were dry, flat, lifeless. There were long periods of no creativity at all. The chatter in my mind became negative and frightening. "This time I've really lost it. I can't write anymore. It's the end of me. I might as well just teach. But, no, I love writing. What's wrong? What's causing this? What can I do about it?" Fret. Fret. Fret.

I was spinning, alternating between a heavy-bodied hopelessness and frenetic pacing and hair twirling. The more I focused on being blocked, the more blocked I seemed to become. In twelve-step addiction recovery programs, members talk about "hitting bottom." I was close to the bottom, if not already there.

One morning I was curled up in my comfy writing chair in front of a crackling fire with an oversized cup of steamy Chai tea beside me. I picked up my new journal with the faint hope that this new and costly leather-bound book with large, crisp, creamy pages might look so appealing to the Muse that she'd swoop down and whisper inspired sonnets into my ear.

I began writing—more moaning and whining about my plight—when I experienced an aha!—a click—a switch had flipped inside me. "Close your eyes and see what the writer inside of you looks like." This didn't sound as strange as it may seem. For years I had worked with visualization and subpersonalities with myself and clients, using imagery to represent the different aspects of ourselves.

I closed my eyes and imagined my office. In sauntered a lively, bright-eyed redhead wearing an early '70's style rainbow-colored flowing skirt and loose-fitting blouse. "I'm Zoe Songbird," she confidently announced. "Oh, no," I remember thinking. "I don't want my inner writer to look like an over-the-hill flower child and have one of those nutty Moonbeam names. I want a Mary Oliver. Refined. Polished. Intellectual, yet soulful." But I knew that the images that present themselves to us, even if not to our liking, are usually instructive. So I decided to at least check her out.

"Susanne," she said. She was intent. "Stop being so hard on yourself. You've had over fifty student papers to read this quarter and you're writing lectures for two new classes. Your creativity is going into school. Relax. It's a cycle. Nothing more than that. You'll see when the last paper is done. You'll be ready to write poetry again. Trust the process."

"God," I said. "You're right. Maybe I'm not finished as a poet. My creative energies have been directed elsewhere." I also realized that I'd written some excellent lectures. Enormously relieved, I was now more receptive to Zoe.

"Why are you appearing in this form?" I asked quizzically. "You must know that this is not how I conceive of myself as a writer."

"I have this wild red hair and colorful hippie appearance because I want to expand your view of your creativity. You're wrapped too tightly in a box. You've forgotten that you also love drawing, using lots of color, and you like to dance, too. Your writing will come alive when you do."

Another bull's eye. I gasped. Zoe was here to stay. Since that time, I regularly interact with Zoe through imagery or in the form of written dialogue. I engage with her when I need direction or inspiration with my writing and, occasionally, just to check in. I have also introduced this simple exercise to many writing clients and participants in writing groups.

Not everyone's writer self is a personified figure. Nor is everyone's imagination visual. One client's writer appeared as a warm sensation in her chest that evoked feelings of hope. Another person's writer was hidden at the back of a dark cave with a fierce dragon blocking the entrance. He discovered that he needed to confront this fiery beast before he could go forward with his writing. The dragon symbolized critical inner voices that carried repeated warnings from the writer's father. He kept hearing that he would end up on the streets if he took time away from his career as a financial analyst to pursue this frivolous hobby.

Some people hear their writer as subtle inner promptings or experience physical sensations such as tingling or changes in bodily temperature. Claude was visited by a snowy white owl named Thomas who would sit on his shoulder at his desk when it was time to write. Simply the reassuring presence of the "guardian owl" helped Claude move into his writing. Incidentally, Claude remembered that the name of his high-school English teacher who encouraged his writing had been Mr. Thomas!

I recommend that people cultivate relationships with their inner writer as they do with important friends. I suggest that they make regular contact, ask meaningful questions, and be open, honest, and direct. For instance: What is the source of this impasse and what can I do to move through it? What direction should my writing take? What will be nourishing for me at this time? I suggest to clients that this be done in a relaxed, receptive state of mind, informing them that I often meditate, stretch or take a brisk walk before doing the exercise.

In response to concerns about the accuracy of the advice, I encourage people to be practical, to use sound judgment as well as intuition. "Try following some of the suggestions and evaluate the results. If your inner writer is not a helpful and trustworthy guide, let her go and get another. It's as easy as that."

> *"I am convinced that all writers are optimists whether they concede the point or not. How otherwise could any human being sit down to a pile of blank sheets and decide to write, say, two hundred thousand words on a given theme?"*
> —Thomas Costain
>
> **Are you an optimist? If so, what are you optimistic about?**

SOME WRITING AFFIRMATIONS

Negative self-talk is a weakness. Positive self-talk is a strength. Cultivate your strength! Replace your doubts with affirmations like the following ones.

* I will write forever. There is no mandatory retirement age.
* Anxiety comes with the territory. I can manage and even embrace my anxiety.
* To write is to allow fortunate accidents to happen. I am open to the next fortunate accident.
* I will astonish myself. Then I'm bound to astonish others.
* A knowledge of beauty is already within me.
* I am interested in my own ideas. That interest is another name for love.
* I can say it well.

✳ I mean to write with integrity.

✳ I am taking up my writing tools.

✳ If I grow quiet, the writing will happen.

✳ I will grow savage and create whole new worlds.

✳ I mean to listen to myself.

✳ I write by myself but with people in mind.

✳ Will they laugh at me? Let them laugh. I'll write anyway.

✳ I will learn my craft by practicing it.

✳ I am mine to make and make over again.

✳ I will stay close to my work. Writing requires intimacy.

✳ I expect gifts. They only come if I keep writing, but then they miraculously appear.

✳ I will create my own culture.

✳ There are infinite ways to fail. So why worry? I'll just write.

✳ I will ask great questions and provide amazing answers.

✳ I will go deeper. Writing means cracking the surface and diving in.

✳ I will be the cream and rise to the occasion.

✳ To write is to improvise. I will become jazz.

✳ Writing is a way to be fully human.

✳ I will write big and let out the immensity inside of me.

Q & A

I have a pretty stubborn, rebellious streak in me. I don't like to conform and I value my freedom and independence. Surely there's nothing wrong with being a freedom-loving iconoclast?

Well, there are a few things wrong. Poorly paid copy editors, editorial assistants, bindery workers, and other publishing employees are turning over a portion of their freedom to help you fulfill your dream of authorship. You don't have to love, honor, and respect them, but probably you should avoid being a hypocrite. You want your freedom, but you also want their services. Are they less worthy than you? Do they deserve to be disrespected? Is there some good reason why you get to be free and they don't?

It is imperative that you remain free and independent, because there are always evils to be unmasked and wrongs to be righted in the world. But it is also important to recognize the ways in which you want and need help from others. You might want to modulate the volume on your demands that you be allowed perfect freedom and the right to every eccentricity. A freedom-loving writer saves the world. But a writer who tramples on others is an unpretty sight. So there are things to think about as you make sense of your natural rebelliousness and your desire to do things exactly your own way.

Self-direction, stubbornness, nonconformity, rebelliousness, and a love of freedom are writers' strengths. Use them honorably.

FOOD FOR THOUGHT

"At the museum a troubled woman destroys a sand painting meticulously created over days by Tibetan monks. The monks are not disturbed. The work is a meditation. They simply begin again."—Susan Griffin
Isn't writing a great meditation practice? Maybe even the greatest?

"I think that we are responsible for the universe, but this does not mean that we decide anything."—René Magritte
Isn't it important to take responsibility for the universe, even if ultimately you decide nothing?

"The true mystery of the world is the visible, not the invisible."—Oscar Wilde
Are you good at just seeing clearly?

"I should compose with utter confidence a subject that set my blood going, even though it were condemned by all other artists as anti-musical."—Giuseppe Verdi
Are you greatly affected by the opinions of others? Or do you remain confident of your own abilities and point of view?

"What release to write so that one forgets oneself, forgets one's companion, forgets where one is or what one is going to do next. Pencils and pads and curling blue sheets alive with letters heap up on the desk."—Anne Morrow Lindbergh
How precious is this release to you? Do you experience it enough?

"There lives in the sculptor's soul something which compels him to imbue his intentions with a heroic boldness and with a joy in achieving monumental effects."—Ernst Barlach
Will you act with heroic boldness and create monumental effects? Why not?

"Our greatest weakness lies in giving up. The most certain way to succeed is always to try just one more time."—Thomas Edison
What gives you the strength to try just one more time? What saps it?

"Art disturbs, science reassures."—Georges Braque
Are you comfortable disturbing people? If not, can you grow comfortable?

"Truth is the god of the free man."—Maxim Gorky
Have you the strength to tell the truth, even if the truth endangers you?

"The overriding thing must be the greatness of the conception, the dark piled-up mass, the trembling light over everything and the fearlessness of the human heart which shows things as they are and likes them that way."—Bertolt Brecht
You can conceive great things. Will you?

"Writing is a form of therapy; sometimes I wonder how all those who do not write, compose or paint can manage to escape the madness, the melancholia, the panic which is inherent in a human situation."—Graham Greene
Aren't writers lucky to be able to escape and even heal themselves through writing?

"Creativity is really the structuring of magic."—Ann Kent Rush
You can structure magic. Will you?

"All things were together. Then mind came and arranged them."—Anaxagoras
Writers have strong minds and strong wills. Are you cultivating those strengths in you?

"And it does no harm to repeat, as often as you can, 'Without me the literary industry would not exist: the publishers, agents, the sub-agents, the sub-sub-agents, the accountants, the libel lawyers, the departments of literature, the professors, the theses, the books of criticism, the reviewers, the book pages—all this vast and proliferating edifice is because of this small, patronized, put-down and underpaid person.'"—Doris Lessing
Can you maintain a feeling of importance even if you're ignored and marginalized?

"The century of airplanes deserves its own music. As there are no precedents, I must create anew."—Claude Debussy
What does the twenty-first century need of its writers? What strengths? What visions?

7
A Writer's Relationships

It is unlikely that a writer will have a career or a decent life until he comes to grips with the fact that relationships matter. Can he hide out in a garret and just write, never striving for intimacy and never looking for marketplace connections, and expect to feel anything less than miserable? Probably not. As important as solitude is for a writer, relationships are equally important.

Furthermore, the distinction between intimate relationship and business relationship is not such a clear one. Your writer friends may be your best business contacts. Your editor may be your prime advocate and supporter. In the contemporary world, where everyone is connected and also easily disconnected, it's not so easy to make perfect distinctions. What is easy to assert is that the task of relating rests squarely on your shoulders.

So, what do you need to do in order to relate effectively to editors, agents, your writing peers, interviewers, publicists, bookstore managers, and other marketplace players, and also to the people closest to you, to your friends and intimate others? Let's begin to answer that question.

> *"I am closer to the work than to anything on earth. That's my marriage."*
>
> —Louise Nevelson
>
> **What are the pros and cons of a life lived this way? Where does intimacy with other human beings fit in?**

Q & A

I've had lots of relationships that, for one reason or another, haven't worked out. But it's more than that. I don't even believe in relationships. Is that a common feeling among writers?

It's a very common feeling. Here's why.

Our culture's prevailing myth about relationships, a myth that's only about a thousand years old but pretty much ubiquitous and unchallenged now, is that each of us should meet someone to settle down with, permanently and monogamously. Together we'll raise a family and live in a regular, prescribed way, ideally on a piece of land and in a house we own, earning a living through the sanctioned work that we do, maintaining ties with and being supported by family and church, and retaining a modest-sized individuality but in most social matters obeying and conforming for the sake of social harmony.

This prevailing myth, and the social rules that go with it, have it that the family is the basic unit of social currency and that permanent dyadic relationships are not only the best and most natural life arrangements but the only ones not suspect. Even feminism, our skyrocketing divorce rate, and other countermyth realities like single-parent families and consciously childless couples have done next to nothing to deconstruct the myth of marriage and family as it has settled in since eleventh-century troubadours began to sing about romantic love.

But writers, male and female alike, have always balked a little (or a lot) at this myth. Concerned about their individual destiny, wanting to chart a course for themselves based on insistent internal demands, needing to speak and to be heard, feeling different from those around them, and asserting that truth-telling, solitude, and nonconformity all possess real value, they have put a priority on realizing their destiny and actualizing their potential, rather than playing out a predetermined role in the social fabric. Not believing, even before postmodernism alerted millions to this possibility, that there are any rules to the game of life except those they arrive at for themselves, writers have typically made less-than-ideal marriage and family material; and they have suffered for this and made others suffer.

For although writers have balked at the conventional ideas of coupling and family-building fostered by society, they have not succeeded very well in inventing their own effective relationship strategies. They have not even mastered what they ought to succeed at best: living alone. Even though writers must accept the possibility that they will be best served by mastering a life alone, a life built on solitude and consisting mainly of solitude, and even though a great many writers live this way as a matter of course, they typically do not understand that living alone can be the right choice, with advantages as well as disadvantages and rewards as well as perils. Because this notion of living alone as a conscious choice has insufficient currency, writers who do live alone often do so guiltily and unhappily, hurt by the worry, stoked by never-ending cultural messages, that to be alone is by definition to be miserable and even diseased.

So writers should consider living alone a real and respectable possibility. On the other hand, a good intimate relationship is far better than living alone. "Good" is the operative word here. Only in given circumstances—

given that two people have a real desire and ability to relate, that they've lived alone and mastered solitude, that they can protect each other's solitude and support each other's deep aspirations, that they've overcome personality deficiencies and learned to manage moods, and that they are ready to work at love because each has good reasons to do that work—will the ground exist for a good, strong, valuable intimate relationship.

Since writers tend to see through the pretty picture of relating as drawn by their culture—since they see clearly that many relationships are struggles in which one or both partners come up losers and that a great many relationships are long-lasting only because both partners have lowered their expectations or lost the wherewithal to leave—they therefore need to provide their own reasons for relating. Given that a writer's goal is not to make a good marriage and settle down but rather to be a writer, given that he or she may well hold the idea of marriage-and-family as overly compromising, given that he or she sees himself or herself as a loner navigating an unknown personal journey—given, in short, that he or she starts out with many potent reasons for not valuing or honoring relating—it is only if and when real reasons to relate present themselves that relating as an idea will begin to make sense.

What are these reasons? The following are a few of them. One is the growing conviction that being alone is too cold and lonely a state of affairs. A second is the realization that forsaking everything for writing is not the only way to frame life. A third is the growing desire to feel less furious, anxious, chaotic, or disturbed—a growing desire, that is, to get well—and the desire to celebrate that budding wellness with another human being. A fourth is the growing willingness to throw open the studio window and let in a breath of fresh air. A fifth is a growing maturity and understanding of the rewards as well as the demands of love.

If reasons like these do not present themselves, if a writer can't open up to new possibilities and instead remains disturbed, armored, and alienated, he or she will remain someone for whom another person is experienced more as a problem than a blessing. But even if a shift does occur, that budding maturity requires attention and affirming. For it is hard and ongoing—but necessary—work to manage the ego and open up to love.

What are the contours of the intimate relationship writers will want to build? Such relationships will rise upon the following twenty building blocks, building blocks upon which each partner in the relationship should stand.

1. Care of each other's solitude
2. Maintenance of emotional security
3. Maintenance of meaning

4. Maintenance of passion

5. Creation of at least occasional happiness

6. A gentle demanding of discipline from oneself and one's partner

7. A gentle exchanging of truths

8. Acceptance of the limits of the human

9. A minimizing of one's own unwanted qualities

10. Support of each other's career and creative life

11. Maintenance of friendship

12. A monitoring of moods in self and other

13. An acceptance of difficulties

14. An acceptance of one's role as ethical witness

15. Management of one's own self, life, and journey

16. Careful communicating

17. A bringing of one's art to the partnership

18. Maintenance of a present and a future orientation

19. Fair treatment of yourself and your partner

20. The creation of a supportive relationship

The ultimate goal for a writer and his or her partner is the creation by two ever-evolving people of a bastion of safety and sanity in a dangerous world, the creation of nothing less than a close-knit unit where each partner defends and enlivens the other, where each respects the other's efforts and has his or her own efforts respected. This fine relating eludes most writers—indeed, eludes most human beings—but it remains the prize upon which we want to keep our eye. This is the long answer. The short answer is that it's natural for writers not to believe in relationships, but a good relationship is still a wonderful thing.

ONE FEMALE WRITER SPEAKS

The following is provided by a writer of my acquaintance:

> *My personal experience has been that heterosexual male artists are put off by my intense, sarcastic, impatient persona. I've had one relationship with a writer and one with a musician. I loved their minds and their tireless verbal skills and their absolute conviction that writing and music were valuable for their own sake. Neither of these men ever asked me why I hadn't sold anything. In the end, though, they both wandered off with sweet, unambitious women. I believe at least one of them said he couldn't keep me and work, too.*
>
> *In my current relationship I see a repeat of some disturbing trends, so I'll use it to try to explain my view of the problem with artist–nonartist relation-*

ships. I met John through business. He'd
been attracted to me for years; he used
to say that I was the most fascinating
woman he'd ever met. We used to have
this standing quarterly lunch date when
we'd talk for hours about everything.
He'd cut out my columns and write notes
and questions on them and fax them to
me at work. He used to beg to read my
novel. I didn't want to get involved with
him because he was actually incredibly
valuable as this kind of remote cheering
section who only saw what I wanted to
show him. All I had to do was be "on" for
a couple of hours every month or so.

But gradually I began to see the
basic dishonesty of holding all the power
and not trusting him. And of course I
wanted to trust him with the other me.
And besides, eventually we were both
between lovers at the same time. But now

> *"Man is the only animal that laughs and weeps, for he is the only animal struck by the difference between what things are and what they ought to be."*
> —William Hazlitt
>
> **How ought things to be in relationships? How are they? Can you get the "is" closer to the "ought"?**

that we're involved he no longer says I'm fascinating. I think sometimes
that I'm pretty repetitive and boring. For the time and effort I put into my
writing I have little to show, which he cannot help but see. I have a tendency
to assign my own negative self-talk to him and then I resent it when he
doesn't say or do anything to reassure me that he doesn't feel that way.
I resent his lumpish inability to intuit when I need that just-perfect two-
word touch that I can deliver when he needs it.

I feel I bring all the emotional intensity to our relationship. It seems like
he just shows up and feeds at the trough. He doesn't have any big life questions he's studying. He's not attempting to raise his consciousness; he thinks
he's okay just the way he is. That's the basic issue. Artists are striving for
something; nonartists buy things. For my part, I feel unlovely and unlovable
and unworthy when I'm agonizing about some piece I can't get right, so
I'm reluctant to write when he's around, so I don't bother; and then I'm not
writing at all, which makes me feel like I'm paying these really big dues
for this relationship and he's not paying anything. And then he'll give me
this look on Sunday afternoon and say, "Don't you want to write anything
today?" Like I haven't passed go for the weekend.

Am I an artist? I'm tap-dancing on the rim of being one. I may be too terrified by the specter of poverty to visit my artist possibilities except in closely guarded and controlled bursts. Let's face it, working full time, being a single parent, and catering to personal relationships limits vegetating time for the soul to ferment art. The women I know who write are all being supported by a husband or a trust fund. They seem to have very little need to stand on their own in the financial world; they have no need for self-sufficiency; no masculine ego drive. I have those things. Having endured a fiscally irresponsible father and then a husband, I don't trust men to take care of me. I don't trust anybody to do that. Rich men make me feel like a collectible; poor men are boring. I don't respect people who don't appreciate the value of money. Money is the chain link fence between dignity and nothingness.

I have a friend who paints the same way I write. We both work full-time and make good livings and try to squeeze our art in between kids and house-cleaning. We agree that our children receive all the unconditional love and most of the patience we have. Our men have to suck it up or move on. Parenting is a whirling vortex of need. If I was a man, I'd avoid women with young children. But despite everything, I'm optimistic. Life is good. My life gets richer, more directed, more intense every year. There has to be a reason I think about and yearn for the things I can't yet name. Though I'm filled with despair sometimes, those times are balanced by other periods when I feel empowered to achieve whatever I want. It must be that I'll have a wonderful relationship some day, probably when I'm ready for it. Meanwhile, I'll keep practicing.

MAKING CHOICES

Your mate would like you to earn some money. She is tired of supporting you. Do you:

    (a) Negotiate for some more time and pledge to write a bestseller?

    (b) Find a job?

    (c) Learn a second profession?

    (d) Plead with her to understand that your writing is important but unprofitable and that she should keep supporting you?

    (e) Find a new mate?

As soon as the person you live with comes out and says that she or he is tired of supporting you, a crisis exists. It can't be swept under the rug; denial will not work. The problem may go away for a week, a month, a year—because your mate feels guilty and retracts her demand, because her job seems a little more bearable the next day, or because she just relents. But the bomb is still ticking. What your mate is saying is either that her work is not satisfying and that she would like the chance to find other work, or that two incomes are really necessary if you and she are to live decently, or that you are not holding up your end of the relationship bargain in some important way and that you don't deserve to be supported. Whatever her reasons, it is unlikely, verging on impossible, that she will be able to tolerate this situation forever.

No doubt this demand will both frighten you and also hurt your feelings. But be careful not to react defensively or run away scared. The best course is to step back and consider the situation. If the relationship is worth maintaining, you will have to find a way to honor her demand. It may be that a little financial contribution will count for a lot, both emotionally and practically. In that case, perhaps you can find a way to teach a few college writing courses, or put your tile-laying skills to good use, or chat with your Aunt Martha about your becoming the first recipient of an Aunt Martha Writing Fellowship. However, a major financial contribution may prove necessary, in which case big questions about a time-consuming day job or a time-consuming second career will have to be broached and addressed.

If the problem is not about money, or only partly about money, then making money will not completely address it. What is in your mate's heart? What's on her mind? Can the two of you talk about the underbelly of the beast? Can you open your hearts and let down your guard? You go first. Tell the truth. Speak. Ask questions. If, when all is said and done, the issue really is money, then money it is. Get some or make some. Find a way to hold up your end of the bargain.

A Little, Light-Hearted Relationship Quiz

A great many writers find relating both painfully difficult and beside the point. The same qualities that make them writers—self-direction, independence, intelligence, skepticism, a love of solitude—also incline them in the direction of isolation, alienation, and a carelessness about relating. This attitude colors both their personal and professional relationships, so that they have trouble with intimacy as well as with marketplace interactions.

If you believe that you are not very well-equipped to relate and not very interested in relating, as many writers believe about themselves, if you believe that your poems or your plays deserve more attention than your mate or your children, that intimacy and relationship are just metaphors and don't stand for anything valuable, that because of your depressions, obsessions, and weirdnesses

> ### *"We're all in this together—by ourselves."*
> —Lily Tomlin
>
> **How do you balance the relational and the existential? Do you admit that they need balancing?**

you're not a very good candidate for relationships, and that, extrapolating from your marketplace difficulties, agents and editors are monsters with whom one can't relate anyway, you are in trouble. This state of affairs needs changing!

Quiz

Take this little relationship test. It doesn't paint so pretty a picture of the writer as relationship whiz; forgive me for perhaps overstating our faults and disabilities. But this is a mirror into which it will pay real dividends to look. Check all the answers that apply. (Hint: most are the wrong answers.)

1. Do you think that you are:
   a. The most important person in the world?
   b. The only person in the world?
   c. Too big to be bothered with relating?
   d. Too busy to be bothered with relating?
   e. Constitutionally unfit to relate?
2. Do you think that, since you are a writer, people ought to:
   a. Treat you like a god?
   b. Treat you like a treasure?
   c. Understand and cater to your needs and whims?
   d. Pay you for daydreaming?
   e. Love you for your potential?
3. When your mate says, "Dear, we really need a car that runs," do you respond:
   a. "You're right, honey. Why don't you work some overtime?"
   b. "Absolutely, darling. I'm virtually certain that in a few more years my psychological fiction which no one currently wants will be all the rage and we can buy two cars and even a dishwasher!"
   c. "When did you become a materialist?"
   d. "What are you saying, that I should stop writing?"
   e. "You're right, sweetie—can't you get a second job?"
4. When your mate says, "Can't you write a bestseller and then write that other stuff?" do you respond:
   a. "Why don't we ask your folks for another loan?"

     b. "Poets don't make money. That's God's first law!"

     c. "But you despise bestseller writing! What's gotten into you?"

     d. "That's like me saying, 'Can't we have sex and then you do the laundry?'"

     e. "All right. I'll try."

5. Do you believe that you and your mate should:

     a. Both be creative?

     b. Both have careers that allow for creativity?

     c. Accept each other's need for solitude and space?

     d. Fight like cats and dogs about who gets to be the creative one?

     e. Agree that only your creativity should be supported?

6. Your mate asks you to "write a little something" for a presentation he has to deliver at work. Do you:

     a. Act like that would kill you?

     b. Complain about the upcoming deadline on your next book?

     c. Reply that that would be beneath your dignity?

     d. Argue that you couldn't possibly write "stuff like that"?

     e. Graciously write it?

7. When you are blocked, do you expect your mate to:

     a. Help in some way?

     b. Sympathize?

     c. Say nothing, but secretly despise you?

     d. Tiptoe around?

     e. Make faces that mean, "What is your problem?"

8. Do you expect your mate to:

     a. Take exactly as much interest in your writing as you take in his/her work?

     b. Take more interest, because your work is more important?

     c. Take only guarded interest, so as not to hurt your feelings by saying the wrong thing?

     d. Take no interest, because he/she can't understand what you're writing anyway?

     e. Act interested, even if he/she isn't, so that you feel supported?

9. With regard to intimacy, are you basically:

     a. Skeptical?

     b. Disinterested?

     c. Too set in your ways to budge?

     d. Too self-involved to try?

     e. Longing for it?

10. What do you see as the value of intimacy?
    a. Regular sex?
    b. Regular conversation?
    c. All kinds of support?
    d. Friendship?
    e. A shared destiny?
11. What good qualities do you bring to intimate relationships?
    a. Some intelligence?
    b. Some empathy?
    c Some honesty?
    d. Some compassion?
    e. A little wildness, passion, and energy?
12. What shadowy qualities do you bring to intimate relationships?
    a. A depressive nature?
    b. An obsessive nature?
    c. An anxious nature?
    d An addictive nature?
    e. Carelessness, big appetites, arrogance, disdain, roving eyes, self-indulgences, a critical nature?
13. When your mate complains about your marijuana use, do you:
    a. Remind her of that old war injury you sustained in grad school and about marijuana's pain-relieving properties?
    b. Remind her that you're growing it, not buying it, and therefore not wasting money?
    c. Show her documented evidence of the link between marijuana and creativity?
    d. Demand to know if she was Born Again while you weren't looking?
    e. Apologize, pledge to stop, and secretly go about your business?
14. When your mate says, "What are you writing?" do you:
    a. Glare?
    b. Wince?
    c. Wave the question away?
    d. Make a feeble, self-deprecating, incoherent attempt at answering?
    e. Just answer?
15. When your mate says, "You love your ideas and your characters more than you love me!" do you:
    a. Exclaim, "Why, that's just what Anna Dostoevsky said about her husband!"?

b. Agree, then duck for cover?

c. Agree, but try to explain yourself?

d. Disagree, run right over, and hug him/her?

e. Pout for about three weeks?

16. When your mate says, "My God, did you buy another book?" do you:

    a. Sheepishly admit it?

    b. Defiantly admit it?

    c. Agree to start attending Bookbuyers Anonymous meetings?

    d. Reiterate that books are sacred objects and that buying them is the only way to get to Heaven?

    e. Reply that you sold a pint of blood on the way to the bookstore and bought it with your own money?

17. When your mate says that he/she would like to live a "normal life," do you:

    a. Roll your eyes?

    b. Look baffled?

    c. Demand a definition of "normal"?

    d. Agree, but have absolutely no suggestions to make?

    e. Graciously chat about the future?

18. Do you like:

    a. Sex?

    b. Sex with lots of different people?

    c. Lots of different sex with lots of different people?

    d. Lots of different sex with lots of different people of different genders and persuasions?

    e. Sex with the same person for fifty or sixty years?

19. Does your day job:

    a. So drain you that you have little patience left for your mate?

    b. So anger you that you come home ready to kill?

    c. So upset you that you stew about it when you might be writing or strolling with your honey?

    d. So demean you that you feel shriveled up and unfit to love?

    e. So depress you that you only want to sleep?

20. Do you have intimacy problems primarily because:

    a. You don't like people all that much?

    b. Books feel more important than people?

    c. Another person with ideas and a will is a problem for you?

    d. People take up too much precious time?

    e. You are pretty unattractive in your habits and ways?

21. Would you enjoy intimacy more if only:
    a. The other person knew exactly when to hang around and when to leave you alone?
    b. The other person was as undemanding as a rock?
    c. You could get your needs met without having to reciprocate?
    d. The other person was a tad more fascinating?
    e. The other person indulged you just a little bit more?

22. What is your recipe for an excellent intimate relationship?
    a. Reasonable person + reasonable person?
    b. Respectful person + respectful person?
    c. Loyal person + loyal person?
    d. Decent person + decent person?
    e. All of the above?

23. Do you treat other writers like:
    a. The enemy?
    b. Dirt?
    c. Rivals?
    d. Your inferiors?
    e. Co-conspirators?

24. When a writer shows you his/her work, do you:
    a. Secretly take it as an opportunity to revenge yourself on the world?
    b. Secretly take it as opportunity to show how much better you are than this writer?
    c. Secretly take it as an opportunity to crush a rival?
    d. Plan to be kind, even at the expense of honesty?
    e. Plan to help, even at the cost of some hurt feelings?

25. A fellow writer asks if he/she can trust you. What do you reply?
    a. "Trust a novelist? You must be mad!"
    b. "I just wrote a self-help book about trust. Maybe you'd care to endorse it?"
    c. "Trust me with what?"
    d. "I'm trustworthy and disloyal. You make sense of that!"
    e. "Yes, absolutely, maybe."

26. Do you see agents as:
    a. Business people who love you if you have something they can sell?
    b. Insulting, mean-spirited, grubby rodents?

      c. Demigods?

      d. Unapproachable, snotty, but invaluable resources?

      e. People?

27. When dealing with an agent, do you see yourself:

      a. On your knees, begging for crumbs?

      b. In a professional relationship?

      c. Still outside, far from the action?

      d. Still a nobody, waiting for the phone to ring?

      e. Better off than if you were out of touch, or avoiding the contact?

28. Do you see editors as:

      a. Bottom-line driven, corporate-minded, arrogant miscreants?

      b. Employees of a business?

      c. Book lovers?

      d. The enemy?

      e. People?

29. When dealing with an editor, do you see yourself as:

      a. One down?

      b. Two down?

      c. Way far down?

      d. In a professional relationship?

      e. At war?

30. Relationships are important because:

      a. They can be really, really useful.

      b. They and only they stand between us and nothingness.

      c. Without them, Kafka was right.

      d. Without them, there is only autoeroticism.

      e. Without them, there is only self-publishing.

Scoring

Please score yourself as follows. If you did not laugh even once, give yourself 6 points. If you cried, subtract 11 points. If you did not recognize yourself in any of the answers, give yourself 22 points. If you think you are good at intimacy and can't figure out why you've been alone for the past fourteen years, give yourself 81 points. If you refuse to talk to agents and editors because they frighten or disgust you, give yourself 144 points. If you have someone to hug, hug that person. If you tallied any points—and even if you didn't—consider making time for love.

> *"Don't forget,*
> *both you and the*
> *editor are putting on*
> *an unceasing act*
> *for the public,*
> *and between you*
> *there should be the*
> *same relation*
> *that exists between*
> *the magician*
> *and his assistant,*
> *off stage."*
> —Jack Woodford
>
> **Do you understand**
> **how you and**
> **your editor are in it**
> **together? But also**
> **at odds?**

THE WRITER-EDITOR RELATIONSHIP

Alan Rinzler is a senior editor at Jossey-Bass and in his career as an editor has worked with some of America's best-known authors. He provided the following piece.

Working with Writers

I started out in my first job as a book editor in 1962. A friend of mine had said to me, "You ought to be in publishing," and also introduced me to her friend Bob Gottlieb, who happened to be the Managing Editor of Simon and Schuster at the time. Since I was just married, about to have a child, and desperate for work, I jumped at the chance and after nine weeks of lobbying, hanging around, and trying to make myself useful, was ultimately hired. I knew nothing about publishing but under Gottlieb's strict but inspiring supervision quickly discovered that I loved working with writers.

"The writer is boss," Gottlieb would say, "and our job is to nurture, support, cajole, recommend, guide when necessary, and get the job done on time. . . . " I took this very much to heart and was thrilled to find myself in the role of gatekeeper, coach, creative nurse, intellectual partner, and—as time passed—stern taskmaster, goad, nudge, nag, and slave-driver. I tried to follow Gottlieb's model: he prided himself on just being "adorable" and doing very little actual editing with his famous writers (who included at the time Joseph Heller, Rona Jaffe, Jessica Mitford, Nicolai Tucci, and Sybille Bedford). But I was a little different, since what stimulated me most was actually jumping into the artistic fray, intervening in the literary process.

Maybe it was because as a beginning editor my writers were not as accomplished and needed more help. Or maybe it was just hubris, just being a pushy young guy. In any case, I wanted to be more involved, to be an active editorial force. Many of my early projects seemed to need a lot of developmental work. Some of my authors, I discovered, needed a tremendous amount of specific literary suggestions regarding characterization, concept,

*focus, structure, and organization. They wanted help in deciding what need-
ed to be added and, especially, what should be cut. Others needed nurturing,
encouragement, reassurance. Some actually seemed to enjoy bouncing
up against me; they liked to fight with me, to be angry and rebel against
my power over their advance payments, against the contractual deadlines,
or in opposition to any judgment of their work as "acceptable" or not.*

*I'd always been an amateur student of psychology. If it weren't for a real
aversion to organic chemistry in my freshman year at Harvard, I might have
stayed pre-med and become a psychiatrist instead of an English major. What
could be more interesting than the development and characteristics of personality and relationships? And who could be more interesting from a psychological perspective than my adolescent heroes and heroines: literary artists!*

*As a book editor, therefore, I was in a unique position to study and play
an active role in the psychological life of many writers. What I observed
and experienced was first of all that writers worked through many serious
emotional issues with their writing. Fiction writers digested, objectified,
revised and ultimately attempted to achieve some mastery over the messiness,
conflicts, and pain of their lives in their stories and novels. They were able
to express their anger, joy, desire, fear—in their work. No matter what
was the reality of their painful experiences with parents, wives, children
(or editors), ultimately they had the last word. Similarly, many nonfiction
writers—like investigative journalists, political activists, self-help gurus—
were also sublimating their rage, resentment, perceptions of abuse, and
visceral yearnings in their work. Many books were conceived and executed,
I discovered, as the perfect revenge, the final dream come true! Clearly
writing was a form of survival, a necessary compulsion, a process of self-
administered therapy for many authors.*

*I also came to appreciate that the act of writing itself, moreover,
was a deeply psychological process. Some writers suffered deeply from
depression and anxiety. Many I knew and worked with were hard drinkers
or abusers of marijuana or cocaine. Writing didn't always come easily.
It required a tremendous amount of solitude, self-discipline, regularity,
even obsessive self-absorption and a kind of continuously renewable
narcissistic self-confidence.*

*Consequently the role of editor, I discovered, usually depended on
the psychological circumstances of the writer: some writers needed a mother
figure to provide "unconditional positive regard"; others wanted someone
to yell at them, to be a stern father figure; a few wanted someone to play
with, to compete against, to tease, threaten, or manipulate like a jealous*

rival. The expectations a writer had of an editor, and techniques for
"getting the job done," ranged from intense utter devotion, to financial
bondage and a kick in the rear.

Eventually I came to see the relationship between the editor and the
writer as a kind of therapy. Given the treatment goal of delivering an acceptable
manuscript, the author, as patient, exhibited powerful feelings of "transfer-
ence" toward the editor, projecting specific needs, revealing strengths and
weaknesses, presenting unresolved conflicts and core relationship problems
from the past in a manner that, if properly interpreted, would show
the editor how to react, what role to play, and what to do to finish the work.

Some of my most interesting and productive relationships were exactly
that kind of dynamic. The role I played for Shirley MacLaine on two of her
books (Out on a Limb and Dancing in the Dark) was very intimate, parental,
encouraging, authoritative—she wanted someone to tell her what to do.
Hunter Thompson (Fear and Loathing on the Campaign Trail, The Great
Shark Hunt, The Curse of Lono), on the other hand, wanted someone to play
with, fight against, but also to be totally responsible for him, like an always forgiving father figure. He wanted someone to say, "It's OK, man," when he screwed
up and also to still love him when he said, "Fuck you, I'm doing this my way."

Some writers wanted (and needed) no personal or disciplinary help
whatsoever (Toni Morrison, Tom Robbins) but appreciated someone to
respond solely on an intellectual and emotional level to their literary issues
and concerns about the commercial business of publishing. Others who
shall remain nameless expected a level of intimacy and commitment which
required me to learn about setting clear limits and boundaries.

Eventually I reached the point where I was able to go back to school.
Times had changed and it was no longer necessary to have a medical
degree and become a psychiatrist to practice as a psychotherapist. In 1988
I finished a master's program in clinical psychology and then spent another
two years interning and getting my license as a Marriage, Family and
Child Counselor (MFCC) in California.

From that point on, I have been able to combine my work as a book
editor with that of a psychotherapist. I work in community mental health,
specializing in crisis intervention and providing psychological services for
victims of crime. I'm Executive Editor for Trade and Psychology at Jossey-
Bass, a San Francisco-based division of Simon and Schuster (back where
I started from), responsible for about fifty books a year that are either for
mental health professionals or for the general public on the subject of psychology. And what I still enjoy most of all is being able to form that intense,

time-limited, goal-oriented, and intimate relationship, that psychological and intellectual partnership for helping writers through the difficult process of delving into their conscious and unconscious to produce: A BOOK!

ROLE PLAY:
Cutting Your Manuscript by a Sixth

Person A: You are a writer whose first book was accepted for publication by A Likely House. You have been working with your editor at A Likely House for a year now, but you've actually only had a handful of conversations with him/her: one or two when the book was first purchased, another when you turned in the first draft of the manuscript (after you turned it in he/she wrote you a long letter outlining the changes he/she wanted, along with marginal notes that he/she provided throughout the returned draft), another conversation in response to the final draft of the manuscript (there were still some major changes that he/she wanted), and another two conversations, one about the book's cover (which you didn't love) and another about the book's title (which they didn't love).

So you've actually talked to this person only half a dozen times, and most of those conversations have had to do with one problem or another. But you believe that your problems with respect to this book are behind you. However, now you receive another "bad news" call from this editor, who tells you that in order for A Likely House to publish the book at the price they think it should carry, the book will have to be reduced in length from ninety thousand words to seventy-five thousand words. Your editor wonders whether you would like to make the necessary changes or whether he/she should. Please consider how you want to respond and also try to notice, as you interact with him/ her, how you would characterize your relationship.

Person B: You are an editor at A Likely House. You purchased a book from this writer about a year ago and now, after much revising, the book is in good shape. Unfortunately, at yesterday's sales meeting, marketing convinced the publisher that the book's planned cover price should be lowered to keep it in line with similar books, and lowering the price means that the manuscript must be considerably shorter than its present ninety thousand words—it needs to be about seventy-five thousand words in length. So you call this writer to break the news to him/her and also to find out whether he/she would like to do the trimming or whether he/she would like to leave the task to you.

Debriefing Questions

Questions for the writer to answer:

1. What was the experience like for you?
2. Did you become any easier with the idea of cutting out a sixth of the book as the conversation progressed?
3. Did you empathize with your editor's plight? Or did you look at the matter from your side only?
4. How would you characterize your relationship with this editor as it unfolded during this interaction?
5. How do an editor's various roles—as publisher's representative, as writer's advocate, as person-with-a-name-to-make—influence and define the editor-writer relationship?

Questions for the editor to answer:

1. What was the experience like for you?
2. How easy or hard would you have found it to be told to cut a sixth of your own book at the last moment?
3. Did you empathize with this writer's plight? Or did you look at the matter only from the side of your publishing house?
4. How would you characterize your relationship with this writer as it unfolded during this interaction?
5. How do an editor's various roles—as publisher's representative, as writer's advocate, as person-with-a-name-to-make—influence and define the editor-writer relationship?

Questions for the observers to answer:

1. What especially struck you about the interaction?
2. What would you have liked to see the writer do differently?
3. What would you have liked to see the editor do differently?
4. To what extent can and should writer-editor relationships survive such difficult moments?
5. How do an editor's various roles influence and define the editor-writer relationship?

SECOND ACTS AND REPAIRED RELATIONSHIPS

F. Scott Fitzgerald once wrote, "There are no second acts in American lives." But I got to have a second act. Here's how it happened.

Jeremy Tarcher, the publisher, purchased a book from me in 1990, a self-help nonfiction book called *Staying Sane in the Arts*. It came out in

1992 and was a critical if not a commercial success (its hardback edition, and later its trade paperback edition, called *A Life in the Arts*, have together sold about 20,000 thousand copies to date). A second book was bought from me, called *Fearless Creating*, which appeared in 1995 and did modestly well, selling 25,000 copies, making some cyberspace bestseller lists, and continuing to sell to this day. These small successes allowed for a third book to be bought, a book called *Affirmations for Artists*, which came out in 1996. It got some nice reviews and fan mail from its readers and sold modestly well. This set the stage for disaster.

> *"The meeting of two personalities is like the contact of two chemical substances; if there is any reaction, both are transformed."*
> —C. G. Jung
>
> **Do you let people transform you?**

I was feeling my oats. I had the ambition to write a book that tied together the latest insights in brain physiology, some research from social and experimental psychology, a little analysis of new genre public art and other activist-art movements, tidbits from postmodern philosophy, and a lot more. My idea was to connect all of this together into a coherent new philosophy of life I called "vitalism" (after an older philosophy of the same name). I wrote a proposal, outlining the book, and it was bought by Tarcher. I called the book *Lighting the Way*.

The only problem was, I couldn't do the subject justice. I read in fields I'd never read in before, trying to master them in weeks instead of years. The deadline I'd set for myself in the contract began to loom and I'd only been reading, not writing. Finally I had to write. But instead of beginning by asking myself the vital question—how could I shape this disparate material into a book wanted by my editor, my publisher, and Tarcher readers?—I just started writing. The chapters I produced looked good enough, but I had the distinct feeling that I was making a big mistake. Still, when I met with Jeremy and his then editor-in-chief, Irene Prokop, for drinks in San Francisco and they asked me how *Lighting the Way* was going, I felt compelled to reply, "It's going great!"

It wasn't. I met the deadline, but at quite a cost. It turned out that I had spent too little time on the book, less than a year from contract signing to finished manuscript, when two or three years were probably necessary. By rushing, I hadn't delivered on the promise of the proposal. I submitted a manuscript that was decent enough, if only you didn't look too closely. But editors and publishers do look closely. Jeremy Tarcher himself called to give me the bad news. The book was unpublishable. It wasn't that it needed massive revisions; it was so far off the mark that no revisions would help. He was kind and cast no blame, but he also didn't equivocate: they were through with the book.

I felt terrible. It isn't easy to forge a relationship with a publisher and I felt sure that I had ruined this relationship by taking their advance money, which they wouldn't recoup, and then writing a bad book. But, although I felt terrible, I at least had the presence of mind to do a few good things. I didn't whine. I didn't complain. I didn't say, "With more editorial care this wouldn't have happened." All I said was, "I hope we can still work together." Jeremy Tarcher and Irene Prokop assured me that we would. But I didn't believe them. I was sure that I had ruined everything.

I didn't believe them when they said that they would still buy books from me, but I took them at their word. Over the next several months I sent them new proposals, each of which they rejected. This confirmed my suspicions. After each rejection I thanked them for their time, more certain than ever that I had killed the relationship with *Lighting the Way*.

Then, in mid-1997, I sent them a proposal for a book called *Deep Writing*. I fully expected them to pass on it, too. But they didn't. The call came early one morning. It amazed me to hear Irene Prokop say that this was the book they had been waiting for all along. Reading just the first sentences of the proposal, she knew that she would buy it. She offered me a nice advance, not quite so large as the one for *Lighting the Way*, but entirely reasonable. I accepted it within the hour.

What did I learn from the experience? To get back on the horse. To keep relating. That even though the bottom line matters, some publishers will give a writer a second chance. That publishing relationships can and do survive mishaps. To keep relating. And that the gods sometimes smile, forgiving an (almost) honest mistake and granting an author a second act in the high drama of writing and publishing.

FOOD FOR THOUGHT

"Never let a domestic quarrel ruin a day's writing. If you can't start the next day fresh, get rid of your wife."—Mario Puzo

Does this irony suit you?

*"The true artist will let his wife starve, his children go barefoot,
his mother drudge for his living at seventy, sooner than
work at anything but his art."—George Bernard Shaw*
Do you agree with this?

*"He who desires to see the living God face-to-face should not seek Him in the
empty firmament of his mind but in human love instead."—Fyodor Dostoevsky*
Do you believe in human love? Would you like to experience some?

*"I've never been able to collaborate with others.
Another person with an idea is a problem for me."—Jackson Browne*
Is another person with an idea a problem for you? Where does that lead?

*"I've always believed in writing without a collaborator, because
where two people are writing the same book, each believes he gets
all the worries and only half the royalties."—Agatha Christie*
Can you collaborate sometimes? In what circumstances?

*"Love begins only when the ego renounces its claim to absolute
autonomy and ceases to live in a little kingdom of desires in
which it is its own end and reason for existing."—Thomas Merton*
Can you renounce your claim to absolute autonomy?

"Competition is for horses, not artists."—Béla Bartók
In what sense must a writer compete? In what sense can
a writer cooperate? With whom and when?

"No play is finished without an audience in attendance."—Mia Dillon
Do you need readers? How will you get them?

*"The applause of a single human being is
of great consequence."—Samuel Johnson*
Can you cultivate at least a little applause? If so, how?

*"Every great and original writer, in proportion as he is great and original,
must create the taste by which he is relished."—William Wordsworth*
How will you help your audience to want what you're writing?
Is audience creation part of your job? If so, how will you do it?

"The audience perceived me in a certain way, and it was in an insecure attempt to please the audience that I lost myself."—Artie Shaw
To what extent do you want to please your audience? To what extent do you want to please yourself? Can you both get pleased sometimes?

"What a mad, inconceivable thing that a writer cannot—in any conceivable circumstances—be frank with his readers."—Herman Melville
Is frankness between writer and reader really not permitted? Why should that be so?

"I have no comrades—no one knows when I need comfort, encouragement, or a grip of the hand."—Friedrich Nietzsche
Who are your comrades? Can agents be? Editors? Publishers? Or are those relationships always bottom-line oriented?

"When you're ambitious, it's hard to be supportive of another person. But it's our job to try, even though it's very hard and one gets jealous."—Squeak Carnwath
What about our fellow writers? How should we deal with them?

"When Pavlova came out to thank the people, this was a moment as great as the dancing itself. It was like a benediction—a blessing."—Muriel Stuart
Are you practiced at saying thank you?

8
A Writer's World

Hello. Welcome to earth. Where are we?

By "a writer's world" I mean the following kinds of entanglements:

 * The characteristics of the majority culture in which a writer operates and how those characteristics infiltrate the psyche. What do *The X-Files*, *The Brady Bunch*, MTV, freeways, malls, freedom of speech, inner cities, the suburbs, thin models, billionaires, nuclear weapons, water filters, fast food, compulsory education, advertising, youth culture, mass culture, computer technology, and all the other cultural elements of our society do to the writer's mind?

 * The characteristics of the subcultures with which a writer identifies: what it means to be an African American and identify with African Americans, a Moslem and identify with Moslems, a woman and identify with women, among other specific kinds of identities. These self-identifications matter personally and professionally: not only may one be an Evangelical Christian who identifies with Evangelical Christians but also a writer published by houses that cater to Evangelical Christians, who appears on radio shows listened to by Evangelical Christians, whose books are reviewed in publications read by Evangelical Christians, and who, for better or worse, is bound up with and beholden to Evangelical Christians.

> *"Each era has its own recipe."*
>
> —Georges Braque
>
> **What is the world like today? What does it require? What recipes are needed?**

 * The economic world: the ways in which people in a particular culture make money—who washes the dishes, who works in the high-rises, who lives in the suburbs, who lives in a cardboard box, what is required to make ends meet, year after year and decade after decade, including especially what is required emotionally, and what all this does to a writer's dream and a writer's reality.

❋ The world of publishing, made up of tiny publishers that produce one or two books a year and the largest houses that offer seven-figure advances to celebrities, the thousands of small and large presses and the people who run them; the world of movie production studios, of actors turned playwrights, and personal trainers turned script doctors; the world of the artistic director, the theatrical season, the main stage, and the second stage; the world of television, the pitch meeting, the summer replacement, ratings, and spinoffs; the world of e-zines and poetry magazines and women's magazines (where, at *Redbook*, ten thousand short stories are rejected for every five published); the worlds of electronic publishing, of high-concept books, of nonbooks.

I mean your world, in short—the world of today's writer.

Let's begin with a little quiz. Can you identify the people who make up the book publishing world? Let's see.

Q & A

Is a copy editor an editor? Who does a freelance editor work for? Who's who in the world of publishing and must I make it my business to figure out their roles and functions?

It is your business, literally and figuratively. So, yes, you should make it your business to identify the cast of characters and usual suspects in the world of publishing.

Who's who in the world of publishing? Sitting alone in your studio, staring at your computer screen, it feels as if the world is made up of you, the writer, and others like you, anonymous and mostly unpublished, along with a huge, amorphous, indistinguishable "them" made up of hotshot agents lunching with up-and-coming editors, celebrity authors and their fast-talking publicists, readers by the thousand lining up to meet their favorite author—all of these folk swirling together in a surrealistic, agonizing vision of good times and laughter, with the laughter at least a little at your expense.

But it's better to get a clearer picture than this. Here are twenty categories of people

> *"And courage, always courage. However lovingly done, the work must be tested in fire."*
> —William Galbreadth
>
> **Are you ready and willing to test your work in the marketplace?**

involved in the publishing world, with a short description of each. Make it your business to understand what they contribute, what they want and need, how they affect you, who they are, and how they're related to you. Consider the functions and responsibilities of the roles they play and the sorts of personality that are likely to go with those functions and responsibilities. Best of all, get to know some of these people firsthand: begin to transform your vision of the publishing world from surrealistic to photo-realistic.

1. Accountant

"Accounting" is a state of mind having to do with maximizing profits, minimizing expenses and losses, keeping an eye on the bottom line, and acting "business-like." "Accounting" plays a role in keeping your advance down but vanishes when a publishing house wants to hold its semiannual sales meeting in Maui or gets the itch to pay a four-million-dollar advance to a celebrity. Everybody at a publishing house acts like an accountant sometimes and refuses to act like an accountant at other times.

2. Acquisitions Editor

The person, whatever her title, who buys books at a publishing house, usually with the advice and consent of others at her house, including the publisher, editor-in-chief, and marketing manager. Her other jobs often include improving the manuscripts she has purchased by editing them, stewarding manuscripts through the publication process, and sorting through the hundreds and thousands of query letters, synopses, proposals, and manuscripts that come her way.

3. Assistant Editor

This may be a junior editor who functions as an editor, buying books and editing books; it may be an administrative assistant who handles secretarial tasks, fields phone calls, and returns phone calls; or it may be a person who does all this. An assistant editor is likely to become a senior editor one day (if she doesn't become a literary agent, book doctor, book packager, or writer first) and already, even in her junior position, is someone who can get a writer's work read by the right people at her publishing house.

4. Associate Publisher

This sort of title, and others like it, refer to a person who has climbed up the ladder in a publishing house and functions as an administrator and manager, minding the bottom line, handling day-to-day crises, and sometimes finding the time to think about the future. But he or she is typically also involved, at least peripherally, in the acquisition of new titles, may still read manuscripts and buy books, demonstrates and generates enthusiasm for individual titles, and usually has a real role in deciding what sorts of books and which individual titles the house will publish.

5. Book Doctor

A book doctor is a freelance editor who tries to turn a book that is currently not strong or publishable into one that is. Her role may also be to help sell the book to a publisher; very often she works with well-known writers who are guaranteed the sale or who have already made the sale but who need (usually a lot) of help in turning their current idea or manuscript into something decent.

6. Book Manufacturer

Book manufacturers, many of whom are in the Midwest or in Asia, are the folks who literally make the books. They are employed by publishing houses and by authors who choose to self-publish, and they can print a few thousand books (or even a few hundred) or zillions. With the new technologies, book manufacturing is changing dramatically; but there will always be someone who fulfills the role of actually making the book.

7. Book Packager

A book packager is a middleman or woman who helps authors put together books, often dealing with the graphics, design, "high concept," and the like, and who presents busy editors with already-strong and even already-manufactured books to add to their lists. Book packagers often associate themselves with highly designed books like coffee-table books, specialty books, and books with lots of photos and design elements, but they may collaborate on any sort of book, being of service (ideally) both to author and editor.

8. Bookstore Manager

Each independent bookstore, each chain bookstore, and even each cyber-space bookstore is managed by someone, and that someone has his or her own tastes. Individual bookstore managers can help make a book successful by prominently featuring it, inviting the author to speak, suggesting it to local reading groups, and overall being a vital part of the enthusiasm that helps given books become successful. You will often find that a book that became a bestseller had the support of an author who micromanaged his or her book by visiting hundreds of bookstores and chatting with hundreds of bookstore managers.

9. Bookstore Events Coordinator

Many bookstores now employ a person whose prime or even sole job is to book authors for book signings, lectures, and other events; the bookstore sometimes shares the expense of the event with the publishing house, but more often than not absorbs the expense as a cost of doing business. Bookstore flyers announcing such events may go out to thousands of customers and serve as an excellent way for potential readers to learn about books. Even if an event is not well attended, a little more name recognition has been garnered for the title.

10. Chain Store Buyer

Chain store buyers determine which books will be stocked system-wide and in what quantities, which featured, and which pushed. The next best thing to Oprah selecting your book for her book club is an appearance by your book in the window of every Borders or Barnes & Noble store nationwide. Since such an appearance is so important in the life of a book, chain store buyers are very influential players in the publishing game.

11. Conference Organizer

To generate sales and publicize their books, writers will often speak at conferences or other events sponsored by professional groups, corporations, and public or private organizations—and their editors certainly hope they will. The conference organizer (or the lecture booker, public events coordinator, corporate events coordinator, or anyone else who arranges for writers to give lectures and workshops) is the person the writer contacts in order to garner an invitation or who invites the writer to speak because his or her work has become known to members of the organization. These speaking engagements can supplement a writer's income in profound ways and turn books that otherwise might sell ten thousand or fifteen thousand copies into books that sell fifty thousand or a hundred thousand copies.

12. Copy Editor

Copy editors are employed by publishing houses. They look at a manuscript after the book's primary editor has done his or her work and the book is considered to be in (nearly) final form. The copy editor works on the book's grammar, but he or she also works on its voice and logic, often peppering the author with scores of questions designed to make the book clearer and more logical. So, although an author may feel as if her book is finished once her primary editor signs off on it, she will still have a copy editor to contend and interact with.

13. Freelance Editor

Freelance editors are sometimes employed by publishing houses, usually as independent contractors on a book-by-book basis and often in a particular area of expertise, and sometimes employed by authors themselves to help get a manuscript in shape for publication. It is rare but not that unusual for an author to hire a freelance editor to help hone his or her manuscript, then get assigned an in-house editor when the book is purchased, and then be assigned yet another editor, a freelancer selected and paid for by the publisher, who works on the book in conjunction with the in-house editor.

14. Literary Agent

Literary agents are primarily salespeople. Of the manuscripts they read, a small percentage, perhaps one, two, or three percent, seem to them salable (which is not the same as good, valuable, or interesting). These they represent. Their sales techniques are extremely simple: they write or phone editors they know personally or have heard of and indicate that they have something the editor may be interested in. Editors, recognizing that agents play an important screening role, tend to respond to these notes and calls relatively promptly. Often an agent is the most valuable person in a writer's professional network; sometimes the writer could do what the agent does, do it just as well if not better, and save the ten or fifteen percent commission agents charge. But the short answer as to whether a writer wants and needs an agent is probably "Yes."

15. Literary Lawyer

Writers have tended to use agents as quasilawyers, employing them to look over the contracts that publishers proffer. Agents put themselves out as being capable of construing and negotiating these publishing contracts, and in general this seems true. But a writer who works as his or her own agent, who has a special copyright law or libel question to answer, who wants a special collaboration contract drawn up, or who otherwise feels in need of a specialist, can turn to literary lawyers, whose numbers are small but who can be found in New York, Los Angeles, the San Francisco Bay Area, and elsewhere, and who can be dealt with long-distance.

16. Publicist

Publicists tout books and authors. Publishing houses have in-house publicists, and writers sometimes also hire freelance publicists on a book-by-book or retainer basis. Publicists attempt to get an author's book reviewed in the print and broadcast media, try to set up author interviews and book signings, and work to get their authors on radio and television. A freelance publicist may charge an author ten thousand to twenty thousand dollars for a single campaign—a campaign which is at its most intense during the six months before a book comes out—or may be hired on a piecework basis and get paid for each interview, review, book signing, or media appearance garnered.

17. Publisher

According to the old saw, mentioned earlier, editors hire writers and publishers hire editors. A publisher is an owner or, in a large publishing house with many imprints, a division manager. At a small house the positions of publisher and acquisitions editor (and even those of publicist, secretary, and other members of the staff) may be held by one and the same person, but even at a medium-sized house the publisher will be one person (often with his or her name on the line of books) and editors will come and go under him/her. Publishers balance the demands of the sales force against the desires of the editors, add and drop titles from the list, and, yes, still acquire new manuscripts themselves, should they come to their attention and catch their fancy.

18. Reader

Every reader has something to tell an author and the early readers of a manuscript—friends, writing buddies, agents—can genuinely help a writer figure out how to improve her manuscript and increase its chances of being sold to a publisher and, afterwards, to readers by the thousands. At its best, the relationship between writer and reader is so intimate and profound that it borders on a love relationship, making readers qualitatively different characters in this otherwise business-oriented cast.

19. Sales Manager/Sales Reps.

The publisher's salespeople are concerned about pricing books competitively, choosing titles, subtitles, sizes, formats, and covers that will sell their books, servicing their accounts, keeping returns of unsold books from stores as low as possible, and in general winning the marketplace game. They tend to predict future performance from past performance, so the fact that a forthcoming book is better or worse than the author's last is hard for them to factor in; they tend to write off authors who don't perform the first time out of the gate. The sales force does not quite dictate to editors or demand that certain books be bought and others avoided, but their influence is enormous and must be reckoned with by editors and authors alike.

20. *Smart and Savvy Buddy*

One of the more important people in a writer's life is a friend with common sense, wisdom, and some understanding of marketing and sales. That friend may listen to the writer's initial ideas and give useful feedback, read the writer's proposals and manuscripts and offer suggestions, and keep on the lookout for publishers interested in what the writer is writing. A good agent also does these jobs, but a smart, savvy buddy can provide a level of intimacy and a continuity of interest that agents rarely can.

> *"In America only the successful writer is important, in France all writers are important, in England no writer is important, and in Australia you have to explain what a writer is."*
>
> —Geoffrey Cotterell
>
> **Where do you live? What are the consequences of living there?**

ROLE PLAY: *Chatting with an Extraterrestrial*

Person A: You are a writer who has materialized on a distant planet. You are in conversation with a friendly extraterrestrial, who is curious about you and your world. You will do everything in your power to satisfy your host's curiosity and explain to him/her/it the real nature of your world.

Person B: You are a wise, sophisticated inhabitant of a distant planet, on which self-knowledge and world knowledge are highly-prized commodities. You as a people have learned to distinguish between reality and illusion, between the important and the superficial, and especially between self-awareness and self-delusion. This writer is visiting from Earth, a planet about which you know next to nothing. Question him/her about the nature of his/her world, asking for clarification on matters you don't understand and not hesitating to point out what you feel are superficial, contradictory, or illusory explanations. Do not stop until you feel as if you have a true, rich understanding of what it's like and what it means to be a writer on Earth.

Debriefing Questions

Questions for the writer to answer:

1. What was the experience like for you?
2. Was it relatively easy or relatively hard to describe the nature of your world?
3. Was it easy or hard to explain the relationship(s) between a writer and his/her culture and world?
4. Do you have any new insights or ideas about the challenges your world provides?
5. Do you have any new insights or ideas about how to handle those challenges?

Questions for the extraterrestrial to answer:

1. What was the experience like for you?
2. Would you like to live on Earth? What sort of place does it sound like?
3. Would you like to be a writer on Earth? Or would you find something else to do?
4. Did you feel that you got a picture of Earth generally or a narrow picture of the writer's particular culture? Did the writer seem "entangled" in that culture?
5. What suggestions do you have that might help this writer free himself/herself from the entanglements of that culture?

Questions for the observers to answer:

1. What especially struck you about the interaction?
2. What did the writer seem to want to focus on? Conversely, what did he/she seem to want to leave out?
3. Did the writer evidence any blind spots? What about the world or the culture isn't he/she appearing to see?
4. What do you see as the entanglements of culture, specifically as they pertain to writers?
5. If you had to briefly describe the nature of the world—say, in fifty words or less—how would you do it?

MAKING CHOICES

You would like to write a book about the year you spent with the Walla Walla Islanders, but you think that it might be wise to find a publisher first. Do you:

    (a) Buy *Writer's Market* and send out query letters to all of the publishers beginning with the letter A (or L for luck, or H for huge advance)?

    (b) Visit a cyberspace bookstore to see what books on the Walla Walla Islanders have already been published?

    (c) Visit a real bookstore to see where books about Walla Walla Islanders are shelved?

    (d) Attend a writers' conference?

    (e) Sit down and think?

The correct answer is (e), don't you think?

We know a lot about the world, if only we would stop and think about what we already know. But our pesky anxiety prevents us from communicating with ourselves. We know, for instance, that a technical book about the Walla Walla Islanders, in which we use the jargon of anthropology and adopt an academic tone, probably needs an academic publisher. For such a publisher to want the book, we probably must have exactly the credentials the publisher is looking for, which no doubt includes a Ph.D. in the field, affiliation with a university, and maybe even the right connections. Do we fit that bill?

> "It will be necessary to yield to the world. What the crowd wants finally becomes law."
> —Georg Philipp Telemann
>
> **Does what the crowd wants become law? If so, what does that mean to you as a writer?**

We also know that very few popular books about Islanders of any sort ever make it into the general arena. Can you name any? So that must mean that large publishers will have a great deal of trouble imagining that there is an audience for such a book. Maybe they can be convinced—but how? If you could legitimately say that Oprah is a secret Walla Walla Islander and wants to come out of the closet as soon as a book on the subject is published, that would turn some editors' heads. But short of something like that, what would convince a large publisher that your book on an obscure culture has any chance in the marketplace?

So you might then say to yourself, "Well, I'm not interested in an academic press (nor would an academic press be interested in me), and I see that

I will have a heck of a time interesting a large, general publisher in my book. But I see specialty books on the market all the time, books on this or that small town, this or that collectible, this or that perennial flower, this or that foodstuff—whole books on carrots, for God's sake! So the smallness of my subject can't be the kiss of death. But who publishes those specialty books? How do they choose which ones to publish? Are they tiny presses with no advances and little distribution possibilities, or are they sometimes medium-sized presses, specialty presses with a built-in audience, or even large presses with a certain kind of mandate? These are things I need to know."

When you talk to yourself this way, you are learning about the world from what you already know about the world. You are taking your raw experiences and turning them into personal knowledge. Traveling to a cyberspace bookstore or a real bookstore is a fine way to begin to research your possibilities, but the first step is to pull out a sheet of paper and a sharp pencil, stay put, and just think. The world is out there but it is also inside your head. Start at home.

Why do we refuse to do this sort of work? Because of pesky anxiety; but especially because we fear the answers. We may well discover that the only publisher in the whole world who might be interested in our book is Walla Walla Island Publishers, whose editor and publisher will only put out a limited edition of five hundred copies and only then if we supply him with a cow and a goat to sacrifice. We dream of bestsellers and great successes and we would rather take a marketing workshop—and not listen to what's being said—than sit down with ourselves and confront the truth. But the truth is a funny, many-sided thing. We may discover that by slanting our Walla Walla Islander story in a certain direction—say, toward magic, shamanism, and the New Age market—we can connect with a major publisher on the lookout for just such a thing. Who knows? The first step is to sit down and consider these possibilities.

THE WORLD OF THERAPY

I thought I'd address my fellow psychotherapists in the following piece. Please do eavesdrop.

Working on Creativity Issues

Important shifts can occur in a single therapy session. It's not because of managed care and a demand for a minimum number of sessions that brief therapy should interest us. There is simply no good reason to suppose that something useful and important can't be accomplished in a handful of sessions or even in a single session. If a conflict that has never before been named were named, examined, and worked through a bit, resistance and all, in the instantly arising relationship between psychotherapist and new client, would even a psychoanalyst say that nothing had been accomplished?

But there's a special sense of "brief therapy" that I'd like to focus on. It is possible to work on creativity issues briefly in each session, checking in on them for a few minutes at a time. You can operate this way with self-identified creative clients, with not-yet-creative clients, but especially with those many "normal" clients who do not bring in any namable creativity issues but who you think would benefit from such work. You can do this brief work at the beginning of a session, signaling that you consider it important, or you can check in at the end of a session, remembering only not to conclude on a down note.

Imagine that you've gotten into the habit of spending five minutes each session on creativity issues with all clients. You actively listen and look for ways to bring such issues up and actively return to them session after session. Consider how this might work with a client you mean to see for six sessions (because that's the number of sessions her HMO will pay for).

The client is an educated professional woman presenting a variety of issues. In the first session you make certain observations and begin to assess and intervene. One thing that you hear is that she minored in English in college, loves to read, has thought about writing, and even has a particular article in mind to write. (You might have gotten this information spontaneously or you might have asked certain creativity assessment questions.) When you wonder out loud whether writing this article might be included as a goal of therapy, you get an ambivalent response.

If you consider the matter of only slight importance, you might drop it there. But if you suspect that your client's reluctance to write may be central and not peripheral—if, say, you see it connecting to anxiety issues or low self-esteem—you might persist and remark that "creativity issues" often turn out to be very important in therapy and that you mean to keep the article in mind and bring it up another time.

During the second session, when you bring the article up again, you will probably learn that she has been thinking about it a lot. What she'll say about what she's been thinking is hard to predict, but that she's been thinking about the article is virtually guaranteed. Depending on her particular response, you might do some educating on the relationship between anxiety and creativity and suggest that she spend a few minutes working on the article in session. There is no better way to bring anxiety and self-consciousness into the room than by inviting such an enactment. If, as may happen, she finds it too difficult to write (providing you with performance anxiety clues *and examples of her self-talk as she tries), you might thank her and praise her for the effort. All of this need not take much more than the five minutes you've allotted to "creativity issues."*

In session three you will probably discover that she is a little angry at you for having subjected her to that in-session writing assignment. Or you may learn that she found the attempt to write in session painful but revealing. If she's agreeable, you might take this opportunity to focus on the value of incorporating a routine into her schedule, so that she begins to devote an hour each day to the article. You might also teach her the affirmation process and work on an affirmation or two that she can use to support herself as she attempts to write this article. Or you might teach an anxiety-management strategy that she can use before starting her writing each day.

In session four you may learn that she was not able to keep to her routine at all and that she hasn't made use of her affirmations yet, but that she did manage to do a little work just before session on the article. You can frame this as a success and an important step in the process, even as you wonder aloud about what waiting until session to write might mean. Together, you might pick a specific goal for the coming week: that, for instance, she work on the article the very next day, whether she wants to or not.

In session five you will learn that she could not get to the article the next day, but that she did work on it three days after the session, and for two days running. But now she's "not sure" that the article is really worth writing. Here you might congratulate her for managing to work for two consecutive days and advise her of the importance of maintaining a "don't know" attitude with respect to the work. This is a time to love the article and to give it a chance, not to criticize it and doubt it.

In session six, your last session together, you might ask for permission to put aside checking in on the article and check in on "creativity issues" more generally. What has she learned about herself? What would she like to pursue with regard to realizing her creative potential? What resources might she employ—say, a class or a writers' group? You might conclude by simply affirming the value and meaning of creativity in a person's life. Probably, at the end of these six sessions, you wouldn't consider your client "transformed" with respect to her creativity issues, but by the same token you'll have done some real work and gotten some important seeds planted.

When you work with a creative client for a longer time, certain questions will keep resurfacing. These include:

* Who am I really?
* Where is the meaning in life?

* What is my role in the world?
* How has my history affected me?
* In what direction should I commit myself?
* What can I do about my moods and anxieties?
* How can I stop making the same mistakes?
* How can I get out of my own way?
* What is my work?
* What prevents me from doing my work?
* How can I choose among creative projects?
* How can I acquire an audience?
* How can I nurture my career?

One week one question must be addressed and the next week another question will demand attention. But over time all these questions will make their presence felt and keep returning, sometimes because they weren't answered the first time and sometimes because a new answer is needed. When therapy lasts for a while, therapists get the opportunity to clarify their client's concerns and questions, investigate historical material that might not have surfaced in brief therapy, patiently monitor the progress of creative projects, and build a solid therapeutic alliance.

> "Some American writers who have known each other for years have never met in the daytime or when both were sober."
>
> —James Thurber
>
> **Does a lot of drinking or drug use go on in your world? Is that all right?**

WRITING BLOCKS

I've saved a discussion of writing blocks for this chapter because writing blocks aren't related to personality alone, or to problems with craft alone, or to any single issue discussed so far. They have to do with the writer's personality, the writer's work, and the writer's world, and especially with how these three interconnect.

An anxious writer working on a difficult novel who also suspects that the novel will not be wanted when it's finished is a candidate for blockage, but perhaps only because all three elements are present. If she weren't so anxious, she might fight through difficulties with the work and forget about her fears about the marketplace. If the work were a little easier, she might be able to deal with her anxiety and her fears about the marketplace. If she were more optimistic about her novel's reception, she might feel more motivated to write, despite her anxieties and the work's inherent difficulties. Things connect; blocks are tangles of interrelated crises and challenges. Therefore I've saved a discussion of blocks and how to deal with them until now.

Since all writers get blocked sometimes, we should each:

1. "Normalize" blockage and assert that what we're experiencing is a universal human experience
2. Attempt to discover and name the causes of our block
3. Provide ourselves with strategies that help us unblock, whether or not we can name the block's cause or causes

Most blocks represent difficulties we're having entering into right self-relationship. In a real sense the problem is not about the work, for even if the work were poorly made or on the wrong track, a person in right self-relationship would simply do the appropriate thing. She would revise the work as needed, or abandon it. In this sense the work doesn't block a person: the block is always in the person.

If difficulties in self-relationship constitute the prime blocker, a second profound blocker is anxiety. Fear—fear of making mistakes, of being criticized, of being exposed, of being proven talentless, of the work never being sold, and so on—is almost always present. To overcome this fear you can work to replace your anxious self-talk with calming self-talk or you can address it in an existential way, reminding yourself about the courage needed to live free. But whatever tactics you choose, your focus on anxiety will prove a profitable one.

But many additional factors contribute to the experience of blockage in addition to core issues like anxiety and failure at self-relationship. If your first three novels haven't sold, that can be a profound blocker. If you live in a noisy environment, with roommates and constant chaos and crises, that can significantly contribute to blockage. When reasons like these cause your writer's block, simply lessening your anxiety or improving your self-relationship will not prove sufficient.

Any of the factors described below may be implicated in a given case of writer's block. Check to see how powerful each may be in your life. Is it a severe blocker, a slight blocker, or not a factor at all? Is it even something of a red herring, masking some more central issue? For instance, is your claim that your visiting in-laws are preventing you from resuming your abandoned novel really the truth? Or is the problem in the novel, whose plot you never believed in? Without some good self-inquiry it will be hard for you to know what the problem actually is.

Factors Contributing to Writer's Block

Creative Process and Work Issues

* An inability to enter into or maintain the awareness state necessary for creative work (caused, for example, by, the inhibiting presence of negative self-talk, doubt, worries, and fears)
* The presence of myths and idealizations (e.g., a misunderstanding of the place of inspiration in the creative process, such that you decide to wait to be inspired before you begin writing)
* A lack of an integrated sense of the creative process (e.g., not understanding to what extent you must become comfortable with "not knowing" what something looks like when you first start out, not understanding how to embrace, rather than battle, the anxiety that attaches to the creative process)
* Skill deficits (e.g., a lack of basic writing skills such that you're never really satisfied with the writing outcome, which leads to meaning drains and blockage)
* Material blocks (e.g., becoming blocked by virtue of the difficulty inherent in the work you're currently doing because the answer to the question you've posed isn't materializing or because the question itself may have been incorrectly framed)
* Pressure paralysis (e.g., blockage arising because you have too many projects going or too many deadlines approaching, or because you perceive your current writing project as unusually important)

World Issues

* Alienation (e.g., a felt separation from the prevailing culture, along with the presence of other outsider feelings—especially that the door to the marketplace is locked, preventing your entry—which gives rise to depression and blockage)
* Feelings of pessimism and defeat (perhaps caused by taking repeated batterings in the marketplace, a failure to make products that feel worthy or that are wanted by publishers, rejection by critics, or other person-and-world failures that lead to a pessimistic outlook and a pervasive feeling of defeat)
* Marketplace issues (e.g., never or only sporadically being paid for your work, a lack of understanding about how to approach the marketplace and "play its games," or an inability to craft a writing career that maintains its momentum)

❋ Issues of showing and selling (e.g., a half-unconscious fear that, were the work to be completed, one would have to attempt to show and sell it, which might result in rejection, failure, and defeat; or the accumulation of many stories written but none published, which is dispiriting, invites doubts about the possibility of success, and acts as a meaning drain)

❋ Role uncertainty (e.g., uncertainty about what you are attempting to do with your creative abilities—to enlighten or to entertain? To be congenial or to be abrasive? To serve as a cultural witness or to gain some popularity?)

Existential Issues

❋ Meaning crises (e.g., suddenly feeling that writing academic poetry, which until this point made use of your ingenuity and cleverness, now seems like a sterile occupation)

❋ Meaning drains (e.g., having your work repeatedly rejected, doing work that feels unrealized, and concluding that your dreams of being a recognized writer will never become reality)

❋ Meaning shifts (e.g., knowing in a corner of awareness that for you writing poetry has become more meaningful than writing prose but fearing that knowledge because of the great investment you've made in writing prose and the great distance you'd have to travel to master poetic forms)

❋ Fear of meaninglessness (e.g., an inability to confront creative work because of fears that in the encounter you'll experience the void or in some other way get a whiff of meaninglessness)

❋ Motivational malaise and existential doubt (e.g., being plagued by doubts about the importance of any work, creative or otherwise, arising from a profound, more central doubt about the importance of your existence or the importance of the existence of the species)

Personality and Psychological Issues

❋ Primary self-relationship issues (e.g., an inability to accept that you must be the central meaning-maker in your own life, or your flight from the responsibilities of freedom)

❋ Psychodynamic issues (e.g., devaluation at the hands of critical parents, anxiety syndromes resulting from dysfunctional family dynamics, or enduring intrapsychic conflicts with regard to self-worth)

❋ Personality trait issues (e.g., excessive manifestation of a useful personality trait like self-direction, which leads to pigheadedness, or a too tame or too wild personality arising because personality traits have combined together in a certain way)

* Fears and anxieties (e.g., fear of negative evaluations, of loss of self-esteem, of exposure, of the unknown, or of failure or success)
* Ego defenses (e.g., the use of ego defenses to protect yourself from unwanted information and unsafe feelings, which leads you to intellectualize about writing rather than encounter the blank page or to fantasize, but not in the service of your creative work)
* Depression (e.g., depression arising for psychological reasons—say, because your parents dismissed your desire to create, placing you to this day in conflict about whether you are entitled to write)
* Addictions (e.g., the long-term use and abuse of alcohol or other drugs, which binds anxiety and covers over pain but ultimately blocks and ruins your ability to be creative)

Culture and Creative Climate Issues

* Repressive childhood (e.g., an anti-intellectual, anti-expressive family attitude, coupled with parental criticism of and punishing responses to your attempts to be creative)
* Repressive adult culture (e.g., belonging to a subculture where creativity is despised)
* Group identifications (e.g., identifying with inhibiting group stereotypes, which you introject and own over time, having to do with lack of intelligence, will-power, skills, or courage)
* A sense of lack of entitlement (e.g., feelings, arising from group or class identifications, or as a result of family myths, that you lack the social or intellectual standing, or you're not lucky enough, to be creative or successful)

Issues of Circumstance

* Day job and second career issues (e.g., fatigue from a taxing day job, anger at having to spend so much time eking out a living, an abiding need to pay attention to your second career leading to increasing investments in your second career and decreasing investments in your writing)
* Relationship demands (e.g., your spouse feeling upset at the time you spend writing, the necessary demands of parenting, or the multiple demands raised by parenting and looking after aging parents simultaneously)

* Particular psychological wounds and traumas relating to writing itself (e.g., receiving especially harsh criticism from a teacher or editor, or producing a kind of work that may have been wanted by publishers previously but is not wanted currently)
* Daily living chores (e.g., shopping, cooking, cleaning the house, doing the laundry, paying bills, answering e-mail—all of which seem endless—or anxiety about all the chores that you're not getting done, like keeping the roses pruned or shopping around for the best auto insurance)

FOOD FOR THOUGHT

"In the republic of mediocrity, genius is dangerous."—Robert Ingersoll
Is quality writing wanted? If not, what does that imply?

"Listen! There was never an artistic period. There never was an art-loving nation."—James McNeill Whistler
If this is no art-loving nation, what will you do?
If no nation is an art-loving nation, what will you do?

"The world doesn't know what to make of originality: it is startled out of its comfortable habits of thought, and its first reaction is one of anger."—W. Somerset Maugham
If originality breeds anger and you are original, what does that imply about the life you'll live?

"The novelist in America is regarded as a kind of freak unless he retreats to the university or hits the jackpot in the mass media."—Harvey Swados
When is teaching a good idea and when is it a bad idea?

"Here, in America, we become virtuosos to gain a name, but there, in the Andean festivals, they try to lose their identity, and they do: they become part of the collective whole."—Quentin Howard
In this culture, is there a collective whole to be a part of? If so, do you want to be a part of it? If not, what does that signify?

"All art is a revolt against man's fate."—André Malraux
What kind of revolt is the writer leading? Is it a sensible one?
Does it matter if it's sensible or not?

*"I am for an art that is political-erotical-mystical, that does
something other than sit on its ass in a museum."*—Claes Oldenburg
How do you get your writing up off its ass so that it causes a stir in the world?

*"My vocabulary was chosen out of the intensity
of my concern."*—William Carlos Williams
What are you intensely concerned about?
What will you write that expresses that concern?

*"It's striking to me how much folk art everywhere has in common. I saw pieces
in Africa that were virtually identical to those I saw in western New Guinea—
or to folk art from Mississippi and Alabama."*—Claudia DeMonte
In what sense is all writing related? In what sense are there real differences
among cultures, genres, and traditions?

*"There are many reasons why novelists write—but they all have one
thing in common: a need to create an alternative world."*—John Fowles
Do you have that need? If so—an alternative to what?

"Fiction, even at its best, is remarkably useless in the world of events."—Wright Morris
What do you think about the world of events? Do you mean to affect it?

*"I get asked to shows—women's shows, black shows—
but I won't be bought until I'm asked to be in shows without
race and gender adjectives in the title."*—Maren Hassinger
In what sense does the world define and label you? Must you get free from
adjectives—as a black writer, woman writer, lesbian writer—revel in them, or what?

*"Painters no longer live within a tradition and so each
of us must recreate an entire language."*—Pablo Picasso
Are you writing in your own idiom and language?
If so, can other people understand you?

"You cannot hide the soul."—Herman Melville
Is the world a soulless place? Or is some soul hiding somewhere?

"What shakes the eye but the mysterious?"—Theodore Roethke
What mysterious things about the world still shake
your eye? Aren't those the things to write about?

9
A Writer's Career

The word "career" has many connotations. It has about it a sense of length and longevity: careers span decades. It has about it a sense of upwardness: one rises in one's career, gets closer to the top, even arrives at the top. It has about it a sense of flexibility and change: in a job you might do the same thing year-in and year-out, but in a career you're likely to be forced to take on new responsibilities on a regular basis.

"Career" also has about it a sense of real remuneration: a career person gets paid and even paid well.

Last but not least, there's the sense of an ongoing need being filled: to be a pilot there must be planes to fly and cargo or passengers needing to get somewhere. So, generally speaking, to have a career you: (1) do something that's wanted, (2) get paid, (3) adapt and change, (4) advance, and (5) stay the long haul.

Does this rough definition of career apply to writers? Yes and no. Since it's possible to make one's name and fortune with one book, movie, or television series, it's possible to "make it" in one's twenties, to be at the bottom on Tuesday and on top by Thursday. The rhythm of advancement is unpredictable and even unnatural. Pay is likewise unnaturally distributed. A poet, writing a thousand fine poems over the course of a lifetime, may be paid virtually nothing, while a television writer, writing with his mind half-shut, can make hundreds of thousands of dollars on episodes that keep repeating themselves in syndication. So pay is weird, very weird, so weird that it can drive writers insane by its weirdness.

Pay and advancement in the writing world are singularly odd. But the other elements of career apply pretty straightforwardly. Each writing world—the worlds of academic presses, regional presses, New York presses, and so on—has its shape and basic requirements, just as TWA, IBM, or Macy's has its shape and requirements. In order to get inside one of these writing worlds and stay there, a writer has to do what's required, sometimes conforming, sometimes risking, but always comprehending what's wanted and adapting to the realities of that environment. Doing what's wanted, adapting, and staying the long haul are three elements of a writing career that any writer could sensibly focus on. Do them well and you have a chance at a writing career.

TALKING TO AGENTS AND EDITORS

"Who wants to be the agent?"

None of the thirty writers moved. Seconds passed. At ten seconds some-one said:

"Oh, all right, if you really need an agent!"

She came up. She sat in one of the two facing chairs. I handed her a tele-phone, which wasn't plugged in.

"Now who wants to be the writer?"

No one moved. Another ten seconds passed. Nervous laughter. To the people in the workshop, it must have felt like days. Finally at twelve seconds someone said:

"Well, I don't *want* to come up!"

But she came up. She seated herself in the chair facing the agent. She fum-bled with the phone I handed her.

Writers at writers' conferences hear agents, editors, and seasoned writ-ers repeat over and over again that a writer's job is part writing and part marketing and sales. They hear that agents and editors are busy people—far too busy to put up with writers who won't or can't present themselves clearly and quickly. Have a high concept. Keep the query letter short. Keep the movie pitch focused. Grab the editor's attention in-stantly, not by the end of the first paragraph but in the very first sentence. Let the agent know what the book's about fast, right now, without any hemming or hawing. Speed! Concision! Faster! Faster!

> *"Editors are extremely fallible people, all of them. Don't put too much trust in them."*
>
> —Maxwell Perkins
>
> Still, you must put *some* trust in them. How much? Of what sort?

Writers hear these things a million times over, hating what they hear, but until they see them enacted they tend simply not to get it. In my performance anxiety workshops for writers, writers get to enact the work of selling. They begin to hear from their peers brave enough to come forward what editors and agents hear all the time: nervous pre-sentations that fail to let listeners know what the work's about. Presentations that do not grab the heart or mind. Painfully inadequate answers to simple questions. Presentations devoid of enthusiasm, because the writer is anxious and hasn't rehearsed.

But how quickly they improve as the role plays progress! When a writer on the third attempt manages to present the plot of her novel in a compelling sentence, everyone smiles. That's it! When the editor asks, "Tell me, what book is yours like?" and the writer is able to respond with an intelligent, vivid comparison, everyone sighs with relief. Excellent! Another hurdle leaped. When the agent asks, "How much of the book is done?" and the writer manages not to reply "I'm sort of just beginning it" but instead asserts "I have the first 20,000 words ready to show," a good feeling courses through the room. We feel that the writer is succeeding, that she's giving herself a chance at success.

Sometimes during a role play an editor or agent will ask a question that not only stops the writer but stops everyone in the room. At one workshop a writer tried to pitch an article on an aspect of disability to a parenting magazine editor. She was doing a fine job of pitching until the editor asked, "What about those people who like to laugh at the disabled?" None of us quite understood what the editor had in mind. After the writer faltered, I asked other writers in the audience to try their hand at answering the question to the editor's satisfaction. Many tried and all failed. What did the editor want? She wanted, she confessed afterward, the following simple thing: to hear the writer say that her article would help re-educate those people.

In the role plays we get to witness failures of communication, missed opportunities, important things left unsaid, things said poorly on both sides, lapses of memory, awkward silences. We hear writers forget the names of their previously published stories and the name of the book they're currently working on. There is no mischief that anxiety will not cause, and we get to witness it all. But by witnessing it, by learning from these workshop experiences, we begin to do better.

My advice to you? Come to my workshop. Better yet, practice. Rehearse. Get a buddy and pitch things back and forth. Sit across from each other, phone in hand.

Ring, ring. Ring, ring.

"Hello, this is the Linda Jones Agency, Linda speaking."

"Yes, good morning. My name is Rosemary Barnes and I wonder if I could just have a few seconds of your time?"

You have a full minute of this agent's time. If you spend it wisely and have the right product to pitch, you'll increase your audience by exactly one. But what a one!

Responding to the Most Natural Questions

Here are some natural questions that an agent might ask you and some bad and good responses:

1. "What have you written before?"

   Wrong: "Well, I guess you saw right through me. I've never been published."

   Right: "I've been writing all my life and I've tried my hand at poetry, short fiction, and essays. This is my first novel, which is complete and in excellent shape."

2. "What's your book about?"

   Wrong: "I couldn't possibly tell you in just a couple of sentences. Let me send you the complete manuscript."

   Right: "It's a historical novel based on a true story of love and cannibalism in the backwoods of Montana. The main characters are Montana's first Buddhist priest and the granddaughter of Abraham Lincoln."

3. "Who's looked at it so far?"

   Wrong: "Some of my friends, who've liked it pretty well."

   Right: "One editor has seen it so far. She thought it was an excellent novel but just not right for her list."

4. "How long is it?"

   Wrong: "It's pretty fat—maybe a shade too long."

   Right: "It's 90,000 words in length."

5. "Who do you see as the audience for your book?"

   Wrong: "People who love good novels."

   Right: "The same people who loved Fanny Mae Smith's excellent *My Brother, My Butcher* and Rita Jo Coolidge's *When Love Comes for Dinner*. I think that readers with an Eastern bent will also be interested in the story, because one of the main characters is a Buddhist priest, and also the many people interested in the life of Abraham Lincoln, who'll be fascinated to hear what happened to one of his granddaughters."

6. "What do you expect to do to support the book?"

   Wrong: "I don't know what you mean."

   Right: "I have a lot of energy, enthusiasm, and marketing ideas. The main thing I'm going to do is look for all the free publicity I can find, talk to bookstore managers about the book, and create as many opportunities to publicize and market the book and help my publisher as I can."

7. "I think I'd like to look at the synopsis and the first fifty pages of the novel. Do you have any questions?"

    Wrong: "Yes. I don't have a synopsis—does that matter? And I'm curious why you charge fifteen percent when some agents only charge ten percent? And you say it'll take you four to six weeks to get back to me—maybe you could cut that time in half? Naturally I'm in a rush to get this book published."

    Right. "No. I look forward to talking with you after you've had a chance to look at the manuscript."

Q & A

Some writers write just a couple of books—or even just one book—and are well known for the rest of their lives. I'm thinking of Harper Lee and *To Kill a Mockingbird* or J. D. Salinger and *Catcher in the Rye*, among others. Then there are writers I've read about who have twenty, thirty, maybe even sixty books published and never make a splash. What does this all mean?

You're asking a few different questions. First, how is it possible to cement one's fame with a single book? Second, how could one possibly not write another book after a successful first book, with all the doors open to you and readers waiting expectantly for your next work? Third, how could a person keep getting published, book after book and decade after decade, if he or she never had a big hit? Wouldn't publishers give up on that writer? Fourth, how could one do all that

> *"What I found myself writing, after the success of my first book, was a second book based on what I thought various people wanted—something fairy tale-like, or exotic, or cerebral, or cultural, or historical, or poetic, or simple, or complex."*
> —Amy Tan
>
> **After something sells, what happens next?**

publishing and not get a big hit? Wouldn't one almost be guaranteed a bestseller if one managed to get into print twenty or thirty times?

The answer to the first question is simple. In this culture, when a book, movie, or song crashes through into general awareness, the waves that it makes are enormous. Not thousands of copies of the book are sold, but millions; not hundreds of thousands see the movie, but hundreds of millions.

Unless one has sold away one's rights to the product—a screenwriter may get a handsome fee but no points in the picture, an author may get a hefty fee for ghostwriting a celebrity biography but no royalties—a fortune is made; and in a culture on the lookout for distractions, a star is born. It is entirely possible to burn in the popular culture firmament forever on the basis of that one hit, remaining forever a celebrity, without having to grant interviews, appear anywhere, or do anything to keep the mystique alive and your book selling.

This sort of stardom is understandable in this culture. But why would such a star stop producing? It might be that the writer has gotten rich and doesn't need the money; but since fortunes vanish and since the writer has to spend her time doing something, it still isn't clear why she would stop writing. I think the real reasons are psychological: that the experience of celebrityhood is disorienting and draining; that the book one launches into after a great success is burdened by the weight of that success, such that the writer doesn't know quite what is wanted or how to compete with that first book, which can lead to the second book being abandoned; that a whole pressing, pulsating world grows up around that first book, a world of fan mail, offers to speak, interview requests, solicitations for good and bad causes, and more, which pulsating world the writer strives to keep at a distance but which has to be handled somehow. Many more could probably be listed. But the point is that for positive reasons—that one has a success and some dollars in one's pocket—and for all the negative reasons just listed, the second book never quite gets written.

The moral is not to avoid success, but that the realities of success are different from what they appear to be at first blush. The same is true for the writer who manages to publish many books. Such a writer has learned that publishers will continue to buy books from him, even though not a single one has become a bestseller, just so long as he picks projects that are wanted by publishers. He knows how to produce a product that will sell or that holds out a reasonable possibility of selling more than the number of copies the publisher believes she needs to sell in order to turn a profit. For a small publisher, that number might be five thousand copies of a hardback with a $22.95 cover price; for a large publisher, it might be twenty thousand copies of a trade paperback with a $16.95 cover price.

Modest sales do hurt writers, and a writer may have lean years where the sales of his previous books so little impress all the editors he deals with that he has trouble selling them on his next projects, even ones they actually like. This is more true for novelists, whose modest numbers are more held against them, and less true for nonfiction writers, whose next "high concept" book may propel them into the ranks of the very successful. But be that as it may, when we see a writer with a lot of credits to her name we know that she has managed to make personal sense of the marketplace time and time again, overcoming modest sales and persevering without a single bestseller. That the bestseller never comes is no surprise; the odds, even for the published writer, are still terribly long. What should surprise us are the resiliency and savvy demonstrated by such a writer, who, after each small publishing victory, has had to reinvent herself and yet again make herself wanted in the fiercely competitive publishing marketplace.

THINKING ABOUT A SMALL PRESS

A writer's career is likely to include a wide variety of publishing opportunities and experiences. You may find yourself published in your college literary magazine, in the letters-to-the-editor page of your local newspaper, in a quarterly literary journal, in a professional journal, in a popular magazine, by a small press, by a medium-sized press, and by a large press, all in the same lifetime. Consider the following, provided by Steve Mettee, publisher of Quill Driver Books and Word Dancer Books, imprints whose titles include *The Portable Writer's Conference*, *The American Directory of Writer's Guidelines*, and other books for writers.

Chance a Small Press?

An old college professor of mine called and asked to stop by the other day. He didn't remember I'd been his student; not that he should, as it'd been close to 30 years.

He was retired now. And in retirement he'd written the book that had been inside him all the years. To him, as with many authors, this book was his child, his tour de force, his stab at immortality.

He brought the manuscript with him—expectantly. He also brought a letter from another publisher, a small independent press like the one I run.

> "*Auntie Mame had circulated for five years, through the halls of fifteen publishers, and finally ended up with Vanguard Press, which, as you can see, is rather deep into the alphabet.*"
> —Patrick Dennis

When you get to the end of the alphabet, what will you do? What are some other techniques and strategies for selling, in addition to sending out query letters to one publisher after another?

"I was elated when I found a press that didn't want to charge me to publish it," he said. "I'd been looking for one for nearly three years." It was only a small press but they had done a few successful books in the same field as his. "There wasn't much money up front but after all the rejections, I jumped at it."

The book, he told me with uncommon candidness, would, once it saw daylight on the bookstore shelves, be recognized for what it was, a brilliant work, subtle and insightful. Fame and paid speaking engagements would follow.

But something had happened.

"I signed the contract, sent in the final manuscript, then never heard from them."

Eight weeks passed without a word, so he called the editor. "After three calls in as many days, I could still only get through to her voice mail. Finally, she called me back and said they hadn't even scheduled a publication date!" She told him they'd call when they had more information.

Another month went by, so he called again. Like the time before, days passed without a return call. "I guess I was starting to get irked."

He wrote the editor explaining he wasn't getting any younger. "I'm 71 now, and would like to see the book in print before I'm pushing up daisies." The letter asked that they let him know where, exactly, the manuscript was in their process and give him firm dates on which he'd see galley proofs and the final book. Eventually the editor called to say they were a small operation and these things took time.

A week or so later he had some cover design ideas and called asking to talk to the press's graphic designer. "I've been living with this book for so long I have a better feeling than anyone for what it should look like." They told him they jobbed this function out and hadn't yet selected a graphic artist for his project. He was surprised, but gave detailed instructions on how he'd like the cover to look to the staff member who had answered the phone.

The following week Dr. Pruitt (not his real name) was looking at Chapter 7 and found that some information in it should be moved to Chapter 3, along with some revisions. He called to let them know the new material would be coming in the mail.

The next month he called and asked to see the publicity and promotion plans for his book. "I was going to be vacationing in a few months and thought we could coordinate plans for book signings and radio and TV interviews, things like that." He was appalled to find they hadn't made any publicity plans yet.

This put him over the edge. He decided a campaign based on the squeaky-wheel theory was in order. He wrote a three-page letter consisting of twenty-four questions to which he felt he deserved answers—immediately.

The letter he brought to show me was the one the editor had included when she returned the manuscript. In it she politely but succinctly explained they didn't have time for this much interaction with their authors. She was sure he would be happier with another publisher. Less than five months had gone by since he'd signed the contract.

His questions for me—which came in a single torrent—were: "Was I wrong for working with a small press? Was it because I didn't have an agent? Would you talk to the editor for me? Or maybe you would read the manuscript to see if you would want to publish it?"

Where did Dr. Pruitt go wrong? What should he have done differently? Or, more to the point, is a small press ever a wise choice? And if you do decide to work with one, what can you do to make things go smoothly?

I have some thoughts and suggestions:

✳ *Yes, small independent presses are a viable alternative today. Because of the solid quality being produced by many independents—and the myriad titles overlooked by the big presses in their search for blockbusters—book reviewers and booksellers are more welcoming of small press output. This means independent presses can get bookstore and library distribution like the big fellows.*

   "But won't I make more money with a large New York publisher?" you ask. Not necessarily. A small publisher's initial print runs are often very close to those of the big New York publishers, and while the advances are often somewhat less, this is frequently compensated for by larger royalty payments.

   Small presses also tend to continue to market books that experience only so-so initial sales. Large publishers have a reputation for remaindering a book that's slow coming out of the chute. They want to focus their resources on what they feel are more promising titles. But keeping a book in print gives the title a chance to take off and a chance to earn more. That a book remains in print is particularly important to an author who, like Dr. Pruitt, plans to use it for back-of-the-room sales at seminars or speaking engagements that might stretch over a number of years.

✳ *Did Dr. Pruitt need an agent? We buy 95 percent of our manuscripts unagented. I think you'll find this to be the case with most independent presses. It is likely the only service an agent could have provided Dr. Pruitt, after the contract was signed anyway, was to convince him to be more patient.*

✳ *I had to tell Dr. Pruitt that I wouldn't read his manuscript. I don't have time to read a whole manuscript to see if it's a book I'm interested in. I, like most editors, prefer a book proposal. A book proposal usually runs a lean fifteen to twenty pages and I need the extra information, such as who makes up the market for this book, what other similar books are out there, how they've sold, and why the author is qualified to write this book, that is included in a well-written book proposal.*

Book proposals are great for authors because you often don't have to write the book before selling it. You just write the proposal. If the book fits my publishing plan and I feel confident with the author, I'll make an offer before there's a full manuscript. Most nonfiction books are sold—to both large and small publishers—this way. For a good step-by-step plan on how to write a nonfiction book proposal, read Michael Larsen's How to Write a Book Proposal *(Writer's Digest Books). If you have already written your book, go back now and write the proposal. I was surprised to find the good professor had sold his book without one.*

✳ *Find out what subjects or genre each press publishes and target your submission to those publishing in the same field as your book's subject. Independents usually have a rather narrow focus. Don't send a book proposal on fly fishing to a press that only publishes entertainment biographies.*

A bit of bad news for those of you writing novels: as yet, most independent publishers only produce nonfiction titles, but the day is coming when a great deal of fiction will be published by small independents. As you or your agent search for a publisher, become familiar with the independents publishing fiction and watch for your opening.

I suspect Dr. Pruitt spent a great deal of the two-plus years it took him to sell his book submitting it to the wrong publishers.

✳ *There are thousands of book publishers in the United States today. If only sixty or seventy turn you down, keep trying. Consider working on a second book while you're waiting for the first to take flight. This helps to keep you in touch with the writing regimen and often helps to take the edge off the anxiety you may be feeling.*

✳ *When you do get a bite, it's okay to ask for a change or two to any contract offered, but don't be too nit-picky. I had one author return my twelve-page contract with sixteen pages of changes. Buried in the scores of details he wanted changed or added was a provision that, in one scenario, he would have the right to buy the books from us at half of our cost to have them printed.*

Since I planned to publish only a trade paperback edition, he wanted to keep hardcover and mass-market edition rights. If I had agreed to this, he would have been free to publish or have published a competing edition of the same book.

To my knowledge this fellow is still looking for a publisher.

✳ *Don't submit the manuscript with spelling mistakes, inconsistent punctuation, or grammar errors. If you're not positive you have the skills to copyedit it, hire a professional. Besides making you look like a rookie, numerous small mistakes slow down the publishing process and place an extra burden on small press editors and their already overworked staffs. Remember, most contracts have an "author must submit a suitable manuscript" clause; the editor may decide your book's not worth the trouble.*

✳ *Abundant mistakes in spelling, grammar and punctuation may put your manuscript at risk, but factual errors are the kiss of death. A small publisher relies on the author to be one hundred percent correct. If an editor, who may not be an expert on the subject, spots a factual error, he'll worry there are more buried within and that, without extensive research and checking, these errors will remain after the book's published. Errors have the chance of both embarrassing the press and negatively affecting sales. See the sentence above concerning the "suitable manuscript" clause.*

✳ *It takes most presses, large or small, nine to eighteen months to get a book in print after the contract is signed. Be patient.*

✳ *Promotion for a title by a small press may be more or less than what a large press would give it, but, with all presses, much of this promo duty falls on the shoulders of the author. Read John Kremer's 1001 Ways to Market Your Books (Open Horizons) and keep the press's publicity people alerted to what you have planned. They will be happy to coordinate with you.*

And Dr. Pruitt? He chose self-publishing, often a practical choice for those with the time, money, and skills required. If you wish to investigate this option, read Dan Poynter's The Self-Publishing Manual (Para Publishing).

A note of caution here: Beware of companies calling themselves "subsidy publishers" or any of the various pseudonyms for vanity presses. If you self-publish, you need a company that refers to itself as a book printer, not a book publisher.

Whatever choice you make, be sure you don't lose sight of the fact that publishing a book is supposed to be a positive experience. Hang loose, hang in there, and have some fun along the way.

MAKING CHOICES

To have a career as a writer, you must:

    (a) Define "career"
    (b) Learn about the marketplace
    (c) Write things that are wanted
    (d) Write millions of words
    (e) Keep bouncing back

The answer, of course, is "all of the above."

How do *you* define "career"? Is it getting one or two books published while you earn a living doing something else—as a scientist who writes the occasional popular science book or as a novelist who teaches writing and beats the odds by getting two of her six novels published? Is it getting a decent percentage of your poetry published while you raise children? Is it climbing some ladder in the world of television, writing a spec episode here and a commissioned episode there, until you find the opening to create and write all the episodes for a hit sitcom, finally making tens of millions of dollars? Is it becoming a famous romance writer and living luxuriously through writing or is it writing category romances that help supplement your family income? In short, how modestly or how grandly do you mean to define "career"?

It will probably hurt your heart to define "career" too modestly—to decide, for instance, that spending a lifetime getting two books written and published that sell twenty thousand copies together amounts to a career. But perhaps not if you otherwise have a satisfying life. If, for instance, you've put together a second career that makes use of your capacities and provides a service so meaningful to others that you do not question why you are providing it, then you may be able to define "career" as "a book or two published in a lifetime" without feeling too badly disappointed. However, if your definition is too modest, you may lose your motivation to write and even forget that you mean to write, as the other things in your life take center stage and push the writing far off into the wings. A modest definition of "career" has its virtues but it also has some undeniable drawbacks.

A very heady, grand definition of "career" has its own virtues and drawbacks. A really grand definition of "career"—the one that secretly defines "successful career" for most writers—is the following one: "I will write one bestseller after another, books (or movies, plays, television series) that are both brilliant and acclaimed, garnering me great financial success and great critical success, changing the lives of millions of people and even the shape of the world, winning me the Nobel Prize (or Emmy, Academy Award, Pulitzer prize) and calls from the producers of television talk shows, as I become like a god in the process." On the plus side, such a definition matches your grandest dreams and keeps the fire of ambition burning, permitting you and even forcing you to keep writing. On the minus side, the odds against your achieving this dream and matching this definition are very, very long; and the danger is that you will break your heart and your mind as, year after year, you find yourself no closer to success as you yourself have defined it.

But however you define "career," and however many times you alter that definition as circumstances and your thoughts on the subject change, you will still have to do steps (b), (c), and (d) listed above to accomplish your goals. For example, you will sell nothing and have no career whatsoever unless you learn about the marketplace. This is a slight exaggeration, and for every ten thousand writers who fail to learn about the marketplace and consequently sell nothing, there will be one who hides out in his attic, writes something intensely personal, drops it in the mail to a well-connected literary agent without even asking for a by-your-leave, and finds in that agent an advocate who sells it in two days flat to an editor at a publishing house with deep pockets for an advance of four hundred thousand dollars. This sort of thing happens. But don't count on it happening. You will exponentially increase your chances of selling if you learn who sells what to whom and why and how.

It will also be better if you write things that are wanted, rather than things that are not wanted. If the things that you want to write are also things that are wanted, that is ideal. If the things that you want to write are not much wanted, then you will have to accept that they are not much wanted and make the best of a bad deal, doing your utmost to find the publishers and audiences that are available. Many writers remain caught on the horns of this dilemma their whole lives, weighing and balancing their desires against the demands of the marketplace.

Whichever way they turn, more toward the idiosyncratic or more toward the commercial, writers will still find that, in general and as a rule, a good book will be easier to sell than a bad book. By "bad" I mean one that fails at the level of craft: a putative romance that doesn't deliver what romances are supposed to deliver, a nonfiction self-help book that offers too little help to too few potential readers and is poorly written to boot, a thriller without some thrills, an experimental novel whose only real experiment is to test whether an agent or editor is patient enough to read more than the first two paragraphs. A first book may be well crafted, but it is more likely that a third or a fourth will be, for writing is really a learning-by-doing process; the prime remedy for poorly crafted work is more work, revising the work at hand or getting on with the next work.

These are all elements of a career. So is resiliency. Writers must bounce back from a million defeats, most of which are internal. When a sentence fails, when an idea vanishes, when a paragraph emerges infinitely uglier than the paragraph one had intended to produce, a bullet is shot into the living dream of writing well. There is that internal barrage; then there are the rounds fired through the mailbox, as rejection letter after rejection letter make its way from agent or editor to one's doorstep. Most of these are just flesh wounds—only a little piece of the heart is ripped away. But they do mount up, until we have hardly any heart left with which to love writing. "Career" has to do with writing and publishing but it also has to do with self-repair: you can't have a career unless you stop the worst of the bleeding and return, bandaged and maybe even healed, to the writing trenches.

> *"I can't imagine getting up in the morning full of enthusiasm to make something that I already made the day before."*
>
> —Carel Visser

A career is made up of many works. Will you repeat yourself? Is that a good thing or a bad thing? What if your audience expects and demands your familiar work?

ROLE PLAY:
Switching Horses in Midstream

Person A: You are a writer on the horns of a dilemma. You've written and had published two "cozy" mystery novels and you could almost certainly sell a third, if and when you wrote it. But you're not sure you want to continue in the role of entertainer, which you feel is the role you're playing when you write these light mysteries. You would rather write a poetic, atmospheric, even spiritual novel about the year you spent in North Africa fifteen years ago, a novel without a shred of dialogue in it and not really "about" anything. You also have a strong desire to write a nonfiction exposé of the Southern Baptist Church, which you belonged to as a child and a teenager. You are discussing this matter with your literary agent, with whom you are on friendly terms. You realize that it's time for you to choose your next project: but how? On what grounds? Which will it be?

Person B: You are this writer's literary agent. You have sold two of his/her mystery novels and they have done modestly well, although his/her editor has confided in you that they have not done quite as well as hoped. You could probably sell that editor a third, but unless this writer has a really excellent seller soon, his/her window of opportunity may close. As you listen to this writer's concerns about his/her next project, do as much reality-testing as you can, letting him/her know that you probably won't be able to handle the literary novel he/she has in mind, as that market is too tight, nor his/her exposé either, as such controversial material is also very hard to sell. What you think he/she ought to do is write a strong third mystery and then really promote it, helping it break off the midlist and into the world of bestsellerdom.

Debriefing Questions

Questions for the writer to answer:

1. What was the experience like for you?
2. How disappointing was it to learn that your agent did not support you in your new choices?
3. Did your feel your friendship for and loyalty to this agent wane as you listened to his/her arguments?
4. What impression did his/her arguments make on you?
5. To whom might a writer turn, in addition to or instead of a literary agent, with help on these kinds of decisions?

Questions for the agent to answer:

1. What was the experience like for you?
2. How easy or difficult did it feel to persistently remind this writer about marketplace realities?
3. Where did you feel your loyalties resting? Were they more with the writer's editor, with whom you hope to do more business, or more with the writer?
4. Could this writer have convinced you that one of his/her less commercial projects was worth representing? What might have swayed you?
5. What most impressed you about this writer's presentation? What least impressed you?

Questions for the observers to answer:

1. What especially struck you about the interaction?
2. With whom did you feel yourself sympathizing more?
3. What thoughts about the marketplace and about your own writing did this role play bring up?
4. What suggestions would you make to a writer who wants to change course in midcareer?
5. Who, in addition to or instead of literary agents, can help writers make these sorts of decisions?

> *"Some reviews give pain. That is regrettable, but no author has the right to whine. He invited publicity, and he must take the publicity that comes along."*
>
> —E. M. Forster
>
> **Do you understand all that you're inviting? Can you name the pains? Can you survive them?**

Nine Cs

Here's a framework for thinking about your life as a writer. The following nine words starting with the letter C paint a pretty complete picture of the challenges you're bound to face.

Character

Each writer is a human being and heir to all the challenges that human beings face. On top of that, you'll also have to contend with the personality issues that, if not peculiar to the creative person, are more pressing in him or her: existential boredom and sadness, depression, personality trait excesses, eccentricities associated with intelligence, self-direction, introversion, conflicts between humanitarian impulses and ego desires, and so forth.

In order for you to lead a self-regulating, creative, authentic life, you will have to wrestle with personality issues at least as much as you wrestle with issues of plotting and characterization. Accept the truth of that and affirm that you are exactly human, nothing more than that but also nothing less.

Calling

How is it that you fell in love with language and books? The question, although it can't be answered, is nevertheless provocative. It points to a vital connection between a person and an art form that is anything but casual and that for many is thoroughly obsessional. Writers turn themselves over to their calling, losing freedom but gaining love, and in the process make powerful investments of self that are bound to lead to pain and disappointments.

Imagine loving something so much, becoming so intrigued by something, or getting caught up so much in the grip of something that you spend a lifetime pursuing it. That is what writers do. To care so much about coaxing beautiful sounds out of strings of words—how strange and illuminating!

If you still love your calling as writer, that is something to remember and affirm. Affirm it by speaking that love out loud:

"I love poetry."

"Novels really do mean something to me."

"I still adore plays!"

But if you're no longer in love with writing, for whatever reasons, then there are only three choices. The first is to abandon writing and look for a new love. The second is to continue with your dull marriage, writing but not loving. The third is to fall in love again. The first choice is dramatic and without guarantees and the second has little to recommend it. The third choice is the one I would ask you to consider: falling in love with your writing again.

The affirmations you might create to rekindle your love could sound like these:

"I will love writing again."

"I will love screenwriting again—this year by starting on an exciting new project."

"It is some aspect of love that I still want to learn about—and only incidentally methods and techniques."

"A chill still runs up and down my spine when I encounter the best that writing has to offer."

Creativity

I am defining creativity as a certain kind of self-relationship rooted in the need to know and do for oneself. It is a self-relationship which demands that you not only solve problems but create problems where none existed before. The average person says:

"Who cares how nature can be abstracted in a sculpture? Why create problems?"

"Who cares if the flute and the harp can play together beautifully? Why create problems?"

"Who cares if you can stage an opera in the woods? Why create problems?"

"Who cares if you can show a dozen perspectives on a small-town racial drama in a documentary film? Why create problems?"

"Aren't shopping for groceries and timing the stock market problems enough?"

The creative person says, "No. I don't agree with that attitude." To support your creative nature, affirm this year that you are a problem-*making* as well as a problem-solving creature.

Capacity

By "capacity" I mean that sense we have that we are or aren't really using ourselves "to our full capacity," as the phrase goes. When we aren't really using ourselves we feel depressed, disappointed, and worse. Last week I began working with a San Francisco theater director who is very busy and looks quite successful, but who came in troubled by her own sense that she was not realizing her potential. The newspapers regularly applauded her efforts, but she felt that she hadn't even begun to work. This is the usual experience of even very productive creative people.

This is a human reality. Also terribly troubling is the fact that so few opportunities exist for the writer to make full use of his capacities. The marketplace is both competitive and demanding of a certain kind of work, which, as often as not, isn't the work that makes one feel really alive. So, it turns out, the creative person is embarked on a lifelong struggle to find and create ways to make use of himself. To do this you may have to challenge yourself more, take new risks, make new marketplace connections, and inaugurate preposterously grand projects.

Control

When we say that someone has an "authority issue" or a "control issue," we are usually speaking pejoratively. We mean that the person "isn't a team player," "doesn't know his or her place," "argues over things unnecessarily," "bites the hand that feeds her or him," "hates to be told anything," and so forth. When we see a writer quarreling with her editor over a minor contractual right and by so doing putting the whole agreement in jeopardy, we suspect that writer "has a control problem."

But every creative person, by virtue of the self-relationship she was born with or subsequently developed, is bound to manifest significant authority, dependency, and control issues. She *is* her own authority, and may fight tooth-and-nail over the smallest matters. She hates feeling dependent, but at the same time craves the financial and emotional support that allows creative work to proceed unhindered by bad day jobs and loneliness. Most importantly, so much feels out of her control that fighting for control—in the wrong places as well as in the right places—becomes second nature.

If a writer can actually control so little—not the Muse, not the work, not acceptance of the work, not the opportunity to work—but at the same time badly needs to be his or her own authority, isn't it logical that he or she will "act up" with putative authorities or have charged feelings about asking for help and depending on others? As you become more aware of these matters, you might want to practice affirmations like the following:

"I can't control the world, but I can acquire wisdom about the world."
"I can't control the goodness of my writing, but I can write every day."
"Independence and interdependence can coexist."

Craft

The idea of craft needs repeated affirming. There is always the doing—the repeated doing over time, the writing and rewriting, the getting better, the letting go of knowing for the sake of really knowing, all of which is connected to doing and yet more doing. Unfortunately there is no necessary linear progression here—one's ninety-ninth story may be better than one's hundredth, and one's first screenplay may have more good ideas in it than one's seventh. But superimposed on that truth is the equally valid truth that one must and should keep learning the elements of one's craft forever.

Affirming the centrality of craft might sound like this:

"I love working at my craft."
"I am continuing to learn about language and ideas."
"Even if I am a master, I am still only an apprentice."

Culture

"Culture" is a big word. You are really and truly embedded in multiple cultures—the publishing world, the world of Tucson or Boston, the world of America, the worlds of advertising and consumerism, and also those worlds with which you happen to identify because you are an African American, a Christian, a Buddhist, a gay, a man, a woman. To loosen the grip of the multiple cultural trances that hold us captive, it is important that you speak about culture out loud.

You might investigate the world of publishing as an anthropologist would. You might investigate the culture of a particular writing genre by attending its annual conference and observing what goes on. You might try to loosen the grip of American culture by reading only Brazilian novels this year, or only African ones. It is not so important which particular aspect of culture you investigate, but rather that you bring the entangling nature of culture into awareness and make mental notes. You can't operate effectively in any culture if you don't know how it operates; and you can't get out of it if you don't know you're trapped in it.

You might want to affirm the following:

"I will keep alert to the ways that culture entangles me."

"This year I will investigate a whole new culture."

"This year I will investigate my own culture, to loosen its grip and better understand it."

Career

Whereas the host of a wildly popular television talk show can almost guarantee that your book will become a bestseller, you can't guarantee your own brilliant career as a writer. But you can identify specific career skills—like what it takes to get on that popular television show.

Why not learn some active listening skills and how to apply them to marketplace interactions? Why not teach yourself some rehearsal and preparation skills, so that you can effectively answer ubiquitous questions like, "Tell me a little bit about yourself?" or "What's your new book about?" Why not teach yourself some anxiety management skills—a breathing exercise, a relaxation technique, or even something esoteric, like learning how to "silently scream"—so that you can have a better shot at achieving your goals and realizing your dreams?

The following are some affirmations connected to career issues:

"I will pay attention to my career."

"I will improve my marketing skills."

"I will learn how the marketplace operates."

Connections

By "connections" I mean all of the relationship issues that we human beings face and that writers often have trouble negotiating smoothly—issues of intimacy, collaboration, cooperation, community. It may be that your most natural state is to be alone, either isolated and distanced from others or, in a better-case scenario, actively engaged in what Voltaire called "a busy solitude." But you also need human contact and intimacy, not to mention support and marketplace advocacy for your ideas and projects. Therefore, you will want to affirm the following:

"I will relate more openly."

"I will watch my own shadow."

"I will collaborate and cooperate."

"I will master connections."

FOOD FOR THOUGHT

*"I think the writer in America doesn't enjoy a very exalted
position: he's really a third-rate citizen."—James Michener*
Can you live a first-rate life as a third-rate citizen?
What would that life include and look like?

*"For every person who will say yes, there are twenty who will say no.
For a positive response you must find the twenty-first person."—Chuck Reaves*
Do you have a plan to survive the hundreds of rejections that come
with a writing career?

*"There's no such thing beneath the heavens as conditions favorable
to art. Art must crash through or perish."—Sylvia Ashton-Warner*
Are you prepared to help your writing crash through? What will you do?

*"The fact is that the intrinsic worth of the book, play or whatever the author is
trying to sell is the least, last factor in the whole transaction. There is probably
no other trade in which there is so little relationship between profits and actual
value, or into which sheer chance so largely enters."—George Bernard Shaw*
Sheer chance notwithstanding, can you improve your odds? How?

*"In a very real sense, the writer writes in order to teach himself,
to understand himself, and to satisfy himself; the publishing of his ideas,
though it brings satisfactions, is a curious anticlimax."—Alfred Kazin*
Are you writing to teach, understand, and satisfy yourself? If so,
can you sense how publication might feel like an anticlimax?

*"One not only writes a book. One lives it. Upon completing
it there are certain symptoms of death."—John Cheever*
What will rejuvenate you after each little writing death?

*"An author who gives a manager or publisher any rights in his work except
those immediately and specifically required for its publication or performance is
for business purposes an imbecile. As 99 per cent of English authors and 100 per
cent of American ones are just such imbeciles, managers and publishers make
a practice of asking for every right the author possesses."—George Bernard Shaw*
Do writers give away their rights because they are imbeciles? Or because it is so
hard to get published?

"In the past I was not so wise as I am now; I left nearly all my business to an agent. I am still encumbered with his slovenly and disadvantageous agreements."—H. G. Wells
No doubt you'll have your ups and downs with agents. What have you learned so far about dealing with them? What can you predict about your future dealings?

"Prose books are the show dogs I breed and sell to support my cat."—Robert Graves, *on writing prose to support his poetry*
Might you need to write one sort of thing in order to support another?

"Manuscript: something submitted in haste and returned at leisure."—Oliver Herford
Do you send out work only when it's ready? Do you know when it's ready? Are you getting better at knowing?

"I don't know whether I like it, but it is what I meant."—Ralph Vaughan Williams
If no one particularly likes what you've written, but it's what you meant to write, what will you do? How will that affect what you write next?

"There've been many, many rejections. If you want to write it your own way, that's the chance you take."—Marchette Chute
Writing it your way or their way is a perennial question. Can you integrate the two ways? Find a middle way? Is that possible? Or desirable?

"I've had it with these cheap sons of bitches who claim they love poetry but never buy a book."—Kenneth Rexroth
After you've "had it," how will you continue?

"As any young artist would, I made all the necessary efforts to enter the system and be recognized by it. Once I was in the system, my only problem was how to get out of it."—Sandro Chia
You want into the system. Might you also want out of it one day? For what conceivable reasons?

"Of the making of books, there is no end."—Ecclesiastes, 12
Are there reasons to stop writing? Are there more reasons to continue?

Afterword

I'd love to hear from you about this book, my other books, the writing process, and the writing life. If you're curious about the individual or group work I do as a creativity consultant or about the lectures and workshops I give, please do get in touch. You can reach me by:

Mail: Eric Maisel, Ph.D.,
      P. O. Box 613,
      Concord, California 94522-0613
E-mail: amaisel@sirius.com
Fax: (925) 689-0210
Phone: (925) 689-0210

Living the Writer's Life is intended to be the first in a series, whose subsequent volumes will look at the lives of creative and performing artists in other disciplines such as music, the visual arts, acting, photography, and dance.

If you'd like to contribute to any of these books, please send me your thoughts, fit into the organizational frame of this book (work, education, craft, personality, challenges, strengths, relationships, world, and career) or any other way you think important, with a one-sentence release indicating that I may use the material. If you like, you can also include a brief resume and an indication as to whether I may use your name (otherwise I won't).

I look forward to hearing from you and learning from you. Thanks!

Index